MUSANDAM

ARCHITECTURE AND MATERIAL CULTURE
OF A LITTLE KNOWN REGION OF OMAN

PAOLO M. COSTA

MUSANDAM

ARCHITECTURE AND MATERIAL CULTURE
OF A LITTLE KNOWN REGION OF OMAN

WITH CONTRIBUTIONS by:
GIGI CROCKER JONES
GERMANA GRAZIOSI COSTA
ROBERT K. VINCENT Jr.

IMMEL
Publishing
LONDON - 1991

ISBN 090715137X

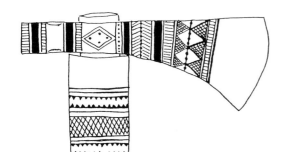

CONTENTS

PREFACE

The Musandam Peninsula, one of the most distinctive features of eastern Arabia and overlooking the Straits of Hormuz with its geopolitical impact for the economy of the western world, has remained to this day virtually unknown. Until a few years ago totally isolated from the rest of Arabia, including the Omani mainland, poor in natural resources and only sparsely populated, Musandam has had only sporadic and limited contact by sea with the outside world. The physical isolation has also been due to the lack of commodities that might attract visitors or conquerors; in turn, this factor has produced a pronounced spiritual seclusion. The consequent unique aspects of the culture of Musandam are at the same time its weakness and charm.

This book is the result of both love and curiosity: partly a psychological response to the touching struggle of people living an unbelievably hard life and partly a more detached interest for the adaptation of man to a very peculiar type of habitat.

The Government of modern Oman has taken a special interest in the development of Musandam: plans have been made, and to some extent already implemented, to create infrastructures and services which continue to improve the way of life for the local people.

This policy has been tempered and guided by cautious attention to the need for preserving regional identity and of course also by the increasing strategic importance of the area.

Modern development will inevitably bring profound change to Musandam and its people. As it happened in so many places of the contemporary world, even here many of the popular traditions will fade away to be replaced by new life-styles. However, memory of original crafts, building styles and techniques as well as the traditional ways of adaptation to the environment, will not be lost, recorded as it is in scholarly works, articles, photographs and films. It is gratifying to know that also this book will form part of those records and contribute to the knowledge and conservation of the Musandam culture.

During the first phase of research the present writer was able to ensure the co-operation of others, equally interested in the region. Their contributions have widened the initial scope of this book and have hopefully made it interesting for a larger audience.

9

Expanding from the original themes on settlement patterns and vernacular architectural forms, the book covers other aspects of the material culture. The contents not only reflect the scope and practical implementation of the research schemes, but also a choice guided by the desire to record the most original contributions of the local communities to the development of the Gulf and Arabian civilization.

The physical aspects of the country, its history, its most typical building forms and the objects made and used in the area should, in the authors' intentions, give the reader various components of a picture which he can put together to enjoy, as they did, the experience of a new discovery.

We have reasons to acknowledge help and support received during the long period of our research in many ways and from many different people, and we have done our best to mention them all here below. We would like to add that our research would not have been possible without the friendly and hospitable attitude of the Musandam people. Contrary to their reputation of hostility and xenofobia, even in the remotest places they opened their houses and let us get acquainted with many aspects of their life. They never showed any hint of hostility, nor even reluctance or unwillingness to co-operate in an investigation which would, we imagined at the time, appear somewhat strange and incomprehensible. It is therefore to the people of Musandam that we dedicate our work.

The present writer and the contributors to this volume wish to acknowledge the encouragement, support and practical help recieved during the whole duration of the research from H.H. Sayyid Faisal bin Ali bin Faisal Al Said, Minister of National Heritage and Culture. Musa bin Mohammed bin Ali al-Wahaibi, then Director of the office of H.E. the Minister of Interior, Kirk Agon, Tim Ash, John Dymond, Peter Sichel and John Sasser should also be mentioned for support and hospitality.

Julian Paxton has kindly undertaken to check the whole text and Angelo Pesce has contributed in many ways to the production. Luciano Couvert has taken part in two surveys and has prepared most of the architectural drawings.

Gigi Crocker has provided information and drawings illustrating the lock systems, and Tor Eigeland has generously let us use some of his photographs.

The many people who helped and supported the research of Mrs. Crocker and Mr. Vincent are mentioned at the end of their contributions.

Photographs are by the authors of the various sections, unless otherwise indicated in the captions.

For Arabic and local names, a simplified form of anglicised transliteration has been chosen, avoiding all those dots and dashes which, on account of the many languages involved, would be unclear to the common reader, and unsatisfactory for the specialist.

Paolo M. Costa

THE MUSANDAM PENINSULA
(detail from *JOINT OPERATIONS GRAPHIC*, scale 1:250.000)

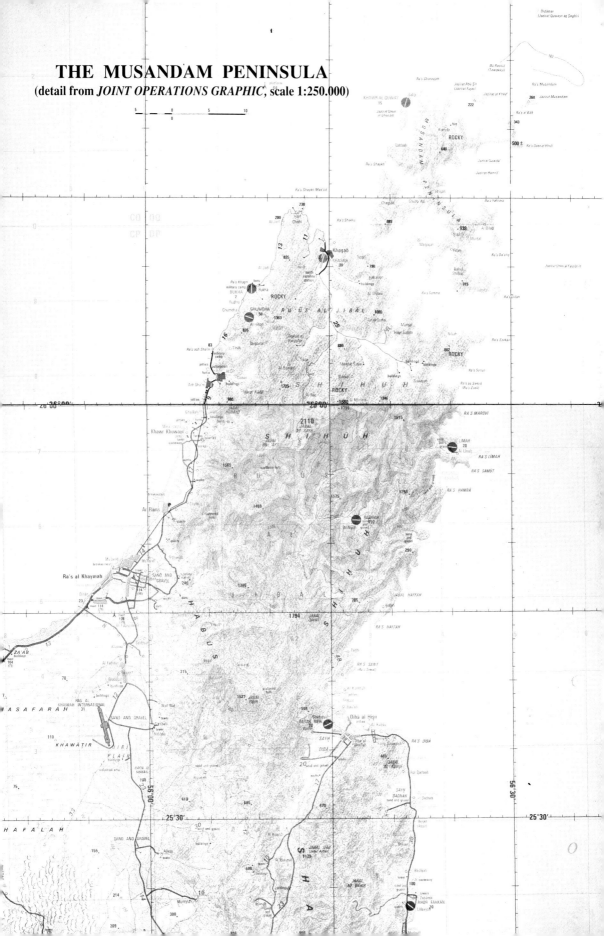

INTRODUCTION

A landmark for navigators, with its towering mountains plunging down sheer cliffs into the sea, Musandam guards the gateway to the Gulf and the northern entrance to the Indian Ocean.

Nobody sailing through the Strait of Hormuz can miss its amazing cluster of headlands and promontories and its spectacular coastline, which in a bare and severe type of environment recalls the fjords of northern Europe.

In this context it may be appropriate to quote the impressions of the Norwegian explorer Thor Heyerdahl approaching Musandam from the upper Gulf at the helm of the 'Tigris', a replica of a Sumerian boat: 'The sky was blue above us, but there were white cloud-banks along the entire horizon ahead. Cloud-banks, but what the devil did we see above the clouds? I grabbed the binoculars....for a moment I could hardly believe my eyes. Above the cloud-banks, raised above the earth was land, like another indistinct world of its own. Solid rock was sailing up there, still so far away that the lower parts seemed transparent and did not even reach down to the clouds; the upper ridge seen against the clear sky was of a different shade of blue.... Were we heading for the Himalayas? Was it an optical distortion, a Fata Morgana?... The whole peninsula was a lofty mountain chain with rock walls dropping almost perpendicularly into the sea...' (Heyerdahl, 1980:175).

A spectacular and impressive coast for anybody sailing through the busiest shipping lane in the world, but also a forbidding land whose rugged terrain has always discouraged any penetration. Until only a few years ago there were no motor roads and only a few precipitous paths, not even suitable for beasts of burden, linked the peninsula to the plains of Ra's al-Khaymah and Fujeyrah. Other steep foot-paths descended from the mountain settlements to the coastal towns and fishing villages nested in the few coves where landing was possible and limited cultivation existed. The towns of Bukha, Khasab, Limah and Bayah were connected with the outer world only by boat.

The difficult terrain has not of course been the sole reason for limited external contact. No easy access to water and the fact that the region does not produce any exploitable commodity of commercial value would have discouraged visitors, traders and conquerors.

In the past the few incursions from the outside world were limited to the establishment of isolated coastal strongholds for the production and support of lines of communication. Traces of a small settlement datable to the Sasanian period have been found on Jazirat al-Ghanim, the northernmost of the islets scattered around the cape. Archaeological evidence is however scanty, which is not only due to the limited research conducted so far, but also, as we shall see later, because of the peculiar geo-morphological history of the region which during the last 10.000 years has been affected by a remarkable subsidence.

At the beginning of the 16th century the Portuguese built a fortified compound at Khasab which became one of their numerous ports of call along the shores of the Gulf and the Indian Ocean.

In modern times few travellers seem to have visited the Musandam peninsula, or even landed on its coasts. The only lengthy description of the region and its inhabitants is by Bertram Thomas who included a section on Musandam in of one of his books (1931:215-254) and also wrote an article in the Journal of the Central Asian Society (1929).

Bertram Thomas and his camel, Khuwara

For a study of Musandam Thomas had undoubtedly the necessary preparation and a keen interest in science and history; unfortunately his outlook and attitude towards the local people and their culture were prejudiced. Gone to Khasab by order of Sultan Taymur bin Faysal to quell a revolt by a local sheikh, Thomas regarded the Shihuh as the enemy. From his headquarters aboard the Sultan's flagship he carried out negotiations with those who had rebeled against the central authority and had almost no contact with the rest of the local population. He was certainly unable - and unwilling - to make journeys into the interior and therefore never saw any of the mountain villages.

Thomas' report became the source of the commonplace repeated by most authors with no direct experience of the area, that the Shihuh are primitive cave-dwellers, or live in pits dug in the ground. At Khasab stories of the life in the interior were told to Thomas either by people who were not from the area and

A sword-dance of the Shiuh

*A group of Shiuh tribesmen
(note axe)*

Shaykh Salih bin Mahdi of the Kumzara

wanted to discredit the locals, or by Shihuh posing as 'modern-minded' emigrés.

Although most of the male population of the larger villages also speak Arabic, the language barrier is one of the main problems which make it difficult to gather accurate information from local people. One must therefore either speak the local language or use a good interpreter.

Interest in the study of Musandam is two-fold: firstly it completes the knowledge of the multifaceted civilisation of the Arabian peninsula and secondly it offers an outstanding example of the adaptation of man to a very peculiar environment. We have already said that Musandam is a cultural island, different from all its neighbours, and the most surprising aspect of the complex cultural scenery of Arabia. The people of Musandam who have their own languages, are not native Arabic-speakers and unlike the other inhabitants of Arabia carry a small axe instead of a dagger: two facts which are the most impressive marks of their identity.

In the present writer's view, the typical mountain dwelling of Musandam instead of being primitive and troglodyte is a sophisticated and unique response of man to a particular habitat. A response which meets brilliantly the need of a special type of life centred on seasonal nomadism. As it will be hopefully demonstrated later in this book *bayt al-qufl* is a refined stone building which forms part of a dwelling conceived to match special requirements for existence in a harsh environment: an architectural achievement which finds no parallel anywhere else in the Near East.

The architecture of Musandam can be divided into two distinct types: the architecture of the coast and the architecture of the mountain. The difference between the two is determined by a number of environmental and socio-economic factors: on one hand are the sites themselves which must be considered in relation with the physical setting, climate, hydrological conditions and the locally available building materials. Equally important are the people, their social organization, economy, lifestyle, and ethno-historic ties.

Northern Musandam lacks the coastal plains which occur further south on both the western and eastern shores of the Oman peninsula. The territories of Ra's al-Khaymah and Fujayrah are in fact mostly silt flats and coastal *sabkha* broken in the hinterland by low hills. To the north, the area which roughly corresponds to the territory under the suzerainty of Oman, starts with an abrupt change of morphology, with the mountains rising higher and extending to the coasts. The sites of permanent coastal settlements and intensive cultivation are in a few bays and limited plains at the mouths of deeply incised wadis.

In the coastal settlements buildings are constructed mainly with coral stones and bricks, palm leaves and beams. As can be expected at coastal sites, a large amount of timber imported from India and Africa is also used in the construction. House forms and decoration display a marked degree of foreign influence which is occasionally noticeable in the use of ideas, motifs and technical solutions, but more often in a kind of eclectic and non-descript character of the building.

The mountain dwelling is a combination of out-of-door areas, covered terraces and verandahs and a type of strongly built house already referred to as *bayt al-qufl*, or 'house of the closure'. This is undoubtedly the most typical construction of the mountain settlements: it should be emphasized however that it is not to be considered simply 'the house' of the Shihuh, but more precisely a component of their dwellings, or simply one of the elements, though the most important, of their living systems.

The Shihuh live in their ancestral mountain villages during the winter season, when the more temperate climate allows an outdoor life, except during the short but torrential rains. Men and flocks then find shelter in the roofed buildings: low byres, chicken pens, verandahs and houses which include the *bayt al-qufl*. The last is however more a store than a living quarter and is in fact the result of local adaptation of the architecture to the semi-nomadic way of life. It responds to the need of creating a building that ensures secure storage of the family possessions, which have to be left unattended for long periods of time.

Bayt al-qufl is built of stones, quarried locally from limestone strata which are very close to surface and tend to split easily into tabular blocks. Only minor retouchments are required to prepare the blocks which are laid in courses with foundations about 1.5/2 m. below surface. The stone and mud roof is supported by rough acacia beams or cantilevered slabs forming a kind of false vault.

Examples of coastal and mountain buildings discussed below will show a number of details of the vernacular architecture.

Building however is only one, though the most impressive, of the many aspects of vernacular material culture which in turn is strictly related to the mentality and cultural identity of the population of the area.

Although the main part of this book concentrates on the study of the built environment, it seemed appropriate to complete the picture of the Musandam culture by including studies on local manufacture of pots, baskets, mats, other objects of everyday use and of course the small axe.

16

Mountain settlement with walled fields (T. Eigeland)

17

The main fort of Bukha

18

Sal al-A'la flats in the lush winter growth

Harf Qabbi (R.K. Vincent jr.)

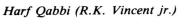

Western coast of the Shamm peninsula from military road on the western side of Wadi Hana. A small stretch of the road running almost at sea level can be spotted on the right (G. Crocker)

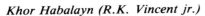

Khor Habalayn (R.K. Vincent jr.)

Boat repairing at Kumzar (G. Crocker)

Modern transport and services in Musandam (G. Crocker)

The western coast of the Musandam peninsula, at Ghumda   (A. Pesce, 1975)

THE COUNTRY AND THE PEOPLE

In a simplified form the outline of the Arabian peninsula appears rather geometric, with a rectangular shape broken at the south-eastern end by a large and irregular protuberance similar to an enormous rhino's head extending its muzzle towards India and pushing its horn deeply into the Iranian coast.

On closer observation however the 'horn', or the Musandam peninsula, is anything but a regularly shaped and pointed tongue of land. From a massive promontory the peninsula develops first into a thin strip of land (the Maqlab Isthmus) and then into an amazing clawlike bunch of irregularly shaped headlands separated by deep fjords and bays and crowned by a string of small islands.

Beside the extremely rugged coastline the other relevant character of the region is the elevation: at 2087m. the Jebel Harim is the highest mountain while the extended plateaux average not less than 800 m. and almost everywhere along the coast the mountains plunge vertically into the sea.

The mountainous character of Musandam explains the name of Ru'us al Jibal (heads of the mountains) which is the proper name of the main body of the peninsula. The traditional geography of Oman describes the northern regions of the country through an anthropomorphic image in which the northern range (al-Hajar al-Gharbi) is likened to a human backbone: the region to the west of it is called the 'back' (al-Dhahirah) and the crescent-shaped plain which lies on the eastern side of the mountains is called 'the stomach' (al-Batinah).

The few U-shaped valleys which furrow Musandam hardly mitigate the severe character of the terrain. The whole peninsula has been affected by a remarkable subsidence: its fjords and bays are in fact the drowned valleys of a region which during the Quaternary has tilted deeply into the sea (Falcon 1973: 1 and 7). According to evidence collected by the Royal Geographic Society expedition, the Musandam peninsula during the last 10.000 years has witnessed a submergence which at the coast may amount to some 60 m. (Vita-Finzi 1973: 420-1). The hinge of the movement may be situated along an ideal line which runs from Ra's al-Sha'm on the western coast to the gulf of Diba on the east (Vita-Finzi, cit.).

Broadly speaking, the habitat of the peninsula can be defined as extremely arid. Sufficient fresh water is available only at a few places on the coast, where the main settlements are located. From the east these are: Diba, Limah, Khasab, Qida, Mukhi, Hana, al-Jadi, Bukha and Ghumda.

Satellite image of the northern tip of Oman

The only large date-palm and fruit tree oases exist at Diba, Limah, Khasab, Qida and Bukha. At the sites of Khasab and Bukha cultivation is almost entirely based on man-made terraces, with retaining walls built to trap the silt washed down by seasonal flooding. Water for irrigation and drinking is supplied by wells from a water table which is only a few feet above mean sea level.

At some places, especially in the large wadi system beyond Khasab where the mountain folds form natural catchment areas, small thickets of acacia are not unknown. They are of two varieties: *Acacia tortilis* (*samr*) and *Acacia ehrembergiana* (*salam*). Large trees of *Ziziphus spina-christi* (*sidr*) and *Prosopis cineraria* (*ghaf*) grow along the wadi bed and sometimes with acacias form small densely wooded areas (Mandaville 1985: 12-17). In one case only, at Sal al-A'la (Wadi Khasab) a large silt plain at the head of the valley supports a real forest covering about 35 hectares with trees reaching the height of 9 m. (Mandaville, cit:15).

Domestic animals include sheep, goats and donkeys. Camels are to be found only in the wadis connected to the sandy plains of the interior. Cows are totally absent and according to B.Thomas 'for inexplicable reasons among the Shihuh Badawin the cow is anathema' (1929:81).

Among the wild animals are mountain leopards, wolves, foxes, hyenas and the small *tahr*, a wild goat (*Hermitagrus jayakari*) unique to Oman. The most common large birds are the Egyptian vulture, the eagle (Bonelli's) and the falcon (Barbary and Sooty) (Gulf Pilot 1967: 2.83; Ghallagher-Woodcock 1980, passim).

As already mentioned, except in artificially irrigated areas, vegetation is extremely sparse, particularly on high ground which consists largely of bare limestone. The intermittent and sometimes torrential rains which occur in the winter season (November to April, peaking December to February) and exceptionally in July-August have caused a severe erosion of the mountains and created in the valleys a detrital fill which can be more than a hundred metres thick.

Over the centuries, retaining walls and terraces have been built at convenient sites to trap silt and control sedimentation where suitable conditions exist for run-off cultivation throughout Oman (Costa-Wilkinson 1987:35). The retaining walls are sometimes of very large dimensions (Falcon 1973, pl. III, b) and create extensive silt field systems (Costa 1983:288, pl.8). Run-off is collected by low deflection walls (called *masaylah*) and directed to the uppermost plot, whence water is distributed to the lower fields by means of spillways or diverting channels. For these patches of intensive cultivation in a bare countryside a matter of concern is the protection against sheep and goats. Outer retaining walls are therefore heightened and made more effective by a crown of thorn branches and the inlets of water conduits are barred by vertical stones.

The autochtonous population of Musandam belongs to three ethnic groups: Shihuh, Kamazirah and Zahuriyn.

The Shihuh form the main part of the population of Musandam and live in the mountains and in all the major coastal settlements where they own gardens or carry out small trade. They are so numerous and widespread that in the eyes of foreigners they epitomize the whole population of Musandam. A few are craftsmen, especially potters and blacksmiths. During the rainy season most of the Shihuh communities, however, live scattered in small mountain hamlets, occupied in animal husbandry (limited almost exclusively to goats) and the cultivation of barley, wheat and lucerne.

The crops are grown solely on run-off irrigation which is dependent on the limited and unreliable winter rains. Such cultivation therefore can rarely produce any surplus for marketing. Only goat breeding is the source of money or bartering with dates, clothing or piecegoods. According to W. Dostal, who has studied the social organization and economy of the Shihuh living in Ra's al-Khaymah, rarely the exchanges of these mountain communities occur beyond the limits of clans belonging to one or a few neighbouring settlements (Dostal 1972).

The Shihuh are divided into two political groups: the Bani Hadiyah and the Bani Shitayr. In all major settlements and coastal towns both groups are present, but in the mountains all inhabitants seem to be related to the Bani Hadiyah.

To the Shihuh confederation belongs the small tribal group of the Kamazirah. As their name implies their centre is at Kumzar, a fishing village nestling in one of the northernmost bays of the peninsula; the Kamazirah are also found at Diba where one of their sheikhs resides, but particularly at Khasab where they own one third of the date palms (Thomas 1929:75) and live in a quarter formed mostly of summer palm-frond houses grouped around the tribal fortified building known as Sur al-Kamazirah (Costa 1985:192). A community of Kamazirah is also to be found on the island of Lark, which is part of Iran. Local oral tradition seems to suggest that in the past the Kamazirah were more numerous, widespread and powerful than are at the present time (Dostal 1972:2).

Located at a distance of less than 50 km. from the Iranian island of Qishm, and with an impassable hinterland which allows no communication even on foot, Kumzar can be considered the most remote and isolated settlement of the Sultanate of Oman. The village is unique in its natural setting, customs and social and spatial organization.

From the tribal point of view the Kamazirah are to be considered Shihuh: this is what they claim themselves (Thomas 1929:75) and is officially recognized (Marshad 1986:60). Ethnically and culturally, however, the Kamazirah are undoubtedly to be regarded as a distinct people. Traditionally they are related to the *Shihi* Bani Shitayr and according to Thomas one of their sheikhs, who habitually resides at Diba, is *de facto* sheikh of the Bani Shitayr confederation.

The social organization is based on the tribe (*qabilah*) which includes a number of clans or extended families (sing. *ahl*). Each *ahl* is divided into family groups (*batina*) formed by single households (*bayt*).

The Kamazirah speak a language of their own, defined by Thomas 'a compound of Arabic and Persian, but distinct from them both' (Thomas 1930:1), but the same author adds that about 20% of the lexicon seems neither Persian nor Arabic in origin, concluding that it is 'a Persian dialect' (op. cit.: 70).

The Kamazirah are almost exclusively fishermen, boat-builders and sailors. Even the limited animal rearing at Kumzar is somehow dependent on the sea: at suitable seasons the flocks are in fact taken by boat to grazing grounds along the coasts of the peninsula and on the islands, particularly the largest of them, *Jazirat al-Ghanim*, commonly called in English 'Goat Island', although the Arabic *ghanim* means goats and sheep collectively.

The third and much smaller group (the Zahuriyn) is to be found in Khasab, on both coasts of the Maqlab Isthmus, on the shores of Dawhat Shisah and in the territory of the town of Bukha. The Zahuriyn are mainly fishermen but work seasonally also in the palm gardens. Their tongue seems to be more strictly related to Arabic (Thomas 1929:74).

Mouth of Wadi Khasab at high tide, near the fort

Helicopter view of the western quarter of Khasab

The bay of Khasab at low tide

Road to Musandam

Inner Wadi Khasab; the silt thins out and gives way to underlying sterile gravels

The end of Wadi Khasab at Sal al-A'la

The southern fringe of the oasis of Khasab

The bay of Qida

Kumzar harbour

Drummer (G. Crocker)

Fayd

Terraced fields at Fayd

35

Mountains and wadis of Ru'us al-Jibal

Mountain village (T. Eigeland)

House entrance at Sal al -A'la

Children playing at Kumzar

Musandam pride (L. Couvert)

Family life at Kumzar: a house overlooking the wadi

39

HISTORICAL BACKGROUND
by Germana Graziosi Costa

The Musandam peninsula, so apparently vital to the control of the Straits and yet, before modern times, such a silent spectator to historic events, occupies a unique position in which its physical character has to a great extent determined its role in the history of the Gulf. During the second half of the 3rd millennium mariners from Sumer sailing down the 'Lower Sea' were struck by the sight of the Kur-Maganna, the mountains of Magan (kur could mean also country, but the first version is more suggestive). What appeared in front of their eyes has been vividly described by T. Heyerdahl who on a reed boat followed the likely course of those ships.

Heyerdahl is a witness to the difficult navigation of such a type of boat along the coasts of Musandam and it is possible that, like him, Sumerian merchants were landing on the Batinah coast of Oman where the currents were naturally taking them. The Batinah offered easier beaches, good supply of food and water and was the outlet of a vast area where mineral resources were exploited.

All the goods sought by the Sumerians were certainly more easily loaded from landing places on the shores of the Indian Ocean or perhaps taken by caravans to the Gulf coast at places like Umm an-Nar (Abu Dhabi) than from the narrow beaches of Musandam.

This reconstruction is however purely conjectural because no systematic and extensive archaeological survey has been carried out and no casual find datable to the 3rd millennium has been recovered so far.

Contacts between Sumer and the countries of Meluhha and Magan went on at least until 1700 B.C.. Meluhha was the region of the river Indus and Magan is now identified with Greater Oman, comprising the modern Sultanate of Oman, the Gulf coasts and possibly also the coast of Iran.

This geographical definition of Magan is interesting because it places Musandam within and not at the margins of the cultural horizon in whose life it was probably involved. In this framework it is possible that the Maka population who gave the name to Makran, also settled on the shores of Musandam: an hypothesis which fits with the survival of an Iranian influence in the Kumzari language and would corroborate a flow of short distance contacts between the inhabitants of the region, and their participation in the social and cultural environment of the lower Gulf.

It is very difficult to reconstruct the pattern of international trade in the Gulf after circa 1700 B.C. The prosperity of Oman seems to continue unchallenged, and archaeological excavations are providing new information for the reconstruction of the regional development which continued in the Gulf area.

It seems that during the 1st millennium the name Magan does not any longer indicate Oman. The name together with that of Meluhha appears at the time to refer to Egypt and Nubia, which were supplying Mesopotamia with the same goods formerly produced by the ancient Magan and Meluhha.

Oman appears in the neo-Assyrian documents with the name of Qade. Historical sources report that Assyrian kings led various expeditions along the Gulf, but did not go further than present Qatar. Although it is reported that a king of Qade, from his home town of Izki travelled to Niniveh to the court of Assurbanipal circa 640 B.C., there is no other evidence of direct relations between the two countries.

Contacts between the opposite shores of the Gulf in the following centuries also remain unclear. Achaemenid reliefs mention the Maka/Maciya people who had a connection with the Indian people and were located 'accross the sea', but this does not necessarily imply that the Maka were in the Arabian peninsula.

D. Potts reviewing all the information available on this problem notes that the word Maka transliterated into Greek with a gamma probably led to the mistaken expression of Gulf of the Magi instead of Gulf of the Maka.

According to Arrian, Alexander's general Androsthenes sent three of his lieutenants along the Arabian coast, but they limited themselves to the exploration of the littoral.

The Seleucid kings maintained an interest in the Gulf trade route which flourished at least during the 4th-3rd century B.C. when Gerrha, a town on the coast that now belongs to Saudi Arabia, occupied an important position. In this period Hormuz, known to Arrian (Harmozeia), and later to Pliny (Armysia) and Ptolemy (Armouza), was the main port at the mouth of the Gulf. If it was part of an independent kingdom of Carmania, as it has been suggested, it is very likely that Hormuz kept contacts with the opposite shores of the Straits particularly when after the 2nd century B.C. most traffic shifted to the Red Sea and Egypt and therefore it felt necessary to strengthen and improve its position.

At the turn of the millennium local traditions and mediaeval historians report the migration of Yemeni tribes of the Malik bin Faham group from SW Arabia to the Gulf. These tribes moved across central Arabia into Greater Bahrein and entered Oman through the Bureimi oasis, or along the southern coast of the Arabian Peninsula and occupied the Omani regions of Ja'lan and the Sharqiyah.

However they did not stop at the Gulf shores, but went over to southern Iran, and the Shihi tradition that claims descent from the Malik bin Faham group is probably an indication of this passage.

The Periplus of the Erithraean Sea written at the beginning of the Christian Era (the date is still very much in dispute) describes in detail the Arabian coast up to the Kuria Muria islands. After this point the country 'being under the control of the Parthians' was inaccessible to the author and since his own course was to Masira and then to India his information becomes less detailed: of the Musandam region he mentions only the cape called 'Asabon' and the existence in the area of pearl fishing. This last information is perhaps not totally precise if referred to Musandam region but pearl fishing was certainly practised along the Gulf coast not only at the time of the Periplus but down to modern times.

It is possible that the Parthians had a foothold on Musandam as well as along the Batinah, as the Periplus says, but no archaeological confirmation of this has been found as yet.

Pliny, writing during the 1st century A.D., seems aware of the difficulty of navigation in the Gulf off the Arabian coastline, particularly because of the 'rocks', almost certainly to be identified with those of Musandam. This meant that beyond Bahrein and Qatif the main sea lanes were nearer to the Persian coast and the passage of the Strait between the Quoins islands and Musandam was avoided because it was too dangerous.

The 3rd century A.D. history of the Gulf is better known. The Sasanian kings having established their power in Iran with Ardashir I (224-247 A.D.) moved towards Mesopotamia, the Arabian peninsula and further south into the Indian Ocean in a strenuous effort to oppose the power and influence of Byzantium as well as to increase their commercial network.

This Persian expansion is partly known through Muslim authors who gave the Sasanian commercial empire the name of Ard al-Hind. An empire in many cases without fixed borders but with firm ties linking merchant communities in distant regions, with far-reaching consequences also in the subsequent diffusion of Islam.

Ardashir made a determined effort to establish his control over the Gulf. He founded for this purpose 11 cities which became so wealthy as to attract Arab raids. These actions forced Shapur II to lead accross the Arabian Peninsula a campaign remembered even in later times for its ferocity. Peaceful activity seems however to prevail in the 4th century A.D. as it appears in the writings of Ammianus Marcellinus: 'There are numerous towns and villages on every coast and frequent sailing of ships'.

The Arab population of Oman was directly involved in the sea trade from the times of Ardashir who employed some Arab sailors in Shihr. His successors held control over Oman first through their vassals, the Lakhmid kings, and later with governors at Sohar and Rustaq and a kind of feudal domination in the interior. A treaty signed at the time of Kusrau Anushirvan (531- 578) regulated the relationship between the Arab tribes and their Sasanian governors. These tribes came from the Malik bin Faham group who had migrated from the western part of the Peninsula some centuries earlier.

Sasanian merchant ships were operating in the Gulf and in the Indian Ocean carrying on a very lucrative trade with India and Ceylon.

The Byzantine emperors Justin (517-52) and Justinian (527-56) made great efforts to secure a hold in the Indian Ocean particularly in order to wrest the silk trade from the Sasanian monopoly. In order to acquire this position they supported the Ethiopians of Axum in the hope that they could act as Byzantine agents in Ceylon which was at that time an important centre for the silk trade.

The Byzantine efforts failed when the Ethiopians were defeated in the Yemen by a local pretender supported by the Sasanians. The result of this struggle was that during the second half of the 6th century A.D. Sasanian control was excercised all along the Arabian Peninsula and some key ports like Aden and Sohar enabled an effective check on the sea lanes to Egypt and Iraq.

In this situation it is more than likely that the Sasanians did not let the Musandam region fall out of their control, a fact that some structures, probably houses streaching along the shore on Jazirat al-Ghanim seem to confirm. The recovery on the surface of diagnostic pottery dates such ruins to the Sasanian period. It is of interest that the closest parallels were made with pottery from sites in the Kerman region, particularly Minab river and Tepe Yahya.

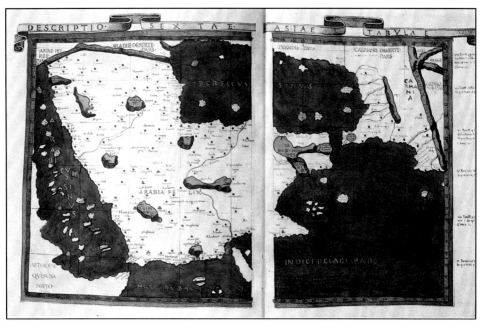

The Arabian peninsula in Ptolemy's map according to Jacopo d'Angelo, Florence 1470

The site has been interpreted as a Sasanian outpost held for its stategic importance. This hypothesis which is based on the consideration that the site must have been unbearably hot in summer, and could be only a military post is not totally convincing and the finds together with a Sasanian potsherd, found near Khasab confirm only, for the time being at least, the existence during the 4th-6th century A.D. of direct contacts with the Persian region.

The trade network established by the Sasanians created possibilities of development in the Gulf. Long distance trade required the control of ports with availability of food, good communications with the hinterland and possibly an easy approach by sea. Other considerations, even water supply, had secondary importance to judge from the cases of Siraf and Hormuz, both developed into thriving ports in later times despite inhospitable surroundings. In any case already in Sasanian times it was the Iranian coast that held a privileged position in the trade. After the entrance in the Gulf it was safer to avoid the rocks of Musandam and to call at ports which offered contacts with the interior.

The Musandam region did not have this asset because its hinterland remained virtually inaccessible, or in any case the journey accross the mountains was too slow to be convenient. The Sasanians preferred instead to hold Sohar which had a rich agricultural hinterland and easy communications along the Batinah and accross the mountains through Wadi al-Jizzi with the Buraimi oasis.

The Musandam region was thus left to a network of regional contacts without entering the flow of international trade.

The Arab tribes of Oman accepted Islam a few years after the Hegira and on their conversion found a reason for unity that enabled them to defeat the Sasanians in 633 in a battle fought on the shores of the Gulf of Oman near the town of Diba (probably to be identified with the region known to Pliny as Dabanegoris Regio) and to occupy the whole country. While these events were taking place the tribes of Musandam also converted to the new religion. The developments of the following centuries clearly show the different role played by the interior and coastal regions of Oman on one side and Musandam on the other.

Oman was in the 8th-10th century A.D. a rich country and the possiblity of exacting from it a large tribute was behind the caliphal expeditions sent to maintain the country in the sphere of the Abbasid control. The expeditions sent from Baghdad landed usually at Julfar (near modern Ra's al-Khaymah); they had then a relatively easy route along the mountain range which led to Bahla and Nizwa which were centres of the political and religious power of the Ibadi Imams. With the occupation of these towns the Abbasid governors could exercise whatever authority they had over the country. Musandam was instead skirted in all the cases of invasion both by land armies and by ships landing support troops on the Batinah coast. No expedition is known to have been sent to submit Musandam, which remained in virtual independence for many centuries.

During the 9th-10th century the trade with the Far East and India was very active. The court of Baghdad was attracting a flow of luxury goods which helped to establish the power of the merchant class. This class had grown on the foundations of the Sasanian trade network represented in the main entrepots of the East by merchant communities which kept ties linking Basra, Oman, India and possibly Africa. Along this network Islam had spread and ports already active before the 7th century became market places where goods were collected, transferred and exchanged.

The towns of Bambhore in India, Sohar in Oman, Siraf on the Persian coast of the Gulf and Basra at the head of the Gulf enjoyed a period of great wealth. With the exception of Sohar and Basra which had good agricultural land, the other towns were surrounded by a barren landscape, but this did not prevent their developement. Sohar and Bambhore were also important oulets of goods coming from the interior, while Siraf and Basra/Ubullah were starting points of important caravan routes leading to the wealthy Fars and Baghdad itself.

The caliphal authority succeeded at that time to impose security on navigation in the Gulf and the success of the Omani fleet sent by Imam Ghassan bin Abdallah (795-822) against Indian pirates extended it to the Indian Ocean.

The internal situation of Oman deteriorated during the second half of the 9th century but not to the point of damaging the prosperity of Sohar, even when at the beginning of the 10th century Arabia was shaken by the Qarmathians. The demand of luxuries at the court of Baghdad was unchanged and the Buweyhid dynasty arising from the military and political position acquired in Baghdad, transformed Fars in its personal base of power, looking at the passage of goods through the Gulf as an important source of income.

Around 972-3 the Buweyhids extended their control to Kerman, Hormuz and Oman and firmly held both sides of the Gulf until they were defeated by the Seljuks in 1062.

Although no contemporary source mentions Musandam specifically it is reasonable to assume that the region was in the sphere of Buweyhid control, particularly when they occupied Hormuz.

The arrival of the Seljuks in the Gulf unbalanced a situation that had lasted quite some time.

The two coastal regions of Kerman and Fars were separated, and while Kerman, and in its wake Oman, prospered under a Seljuk dynasty, Fars fell in a state of disorder under the raids of Shabankara'i tribesmen.

In this situation the demand for luxury goods from the upper Gulf diminished and the trade from the Indian Ocean tended to stop at the head of the Gulf to the advantage of Omani ports and particularly of Hormuz, so that the merchants from Qais (probably of Sirafi origin) had to resort to force in order to divert some of the goods destined for Kerman and central Iran to Qais for their own profit. This struggle, described as piracy, involved also the Arab coast of the Gulf. Qais became the economic outlet of Fars when the region was pacified under the local dinasty of the Salghurids, and was able to extend its control over Bahrein, Qatif, Tarut and Ahsa, while Oman remained more or less tied to the political situation of Kerman.

During the 13th century Hormuz emerged as an important trade centre, and under the leadership of Mahmud Qalhati around the middle of the century became virtually independent from the Mongol rulers of Kerman and slowly overpowered Qais.

The indipendence of the town was strengthened when the population moved to the island of Jerun and fortified the settlement which retained the name of Hormuz. The physical detachment from the mainland enabled the dynasty of

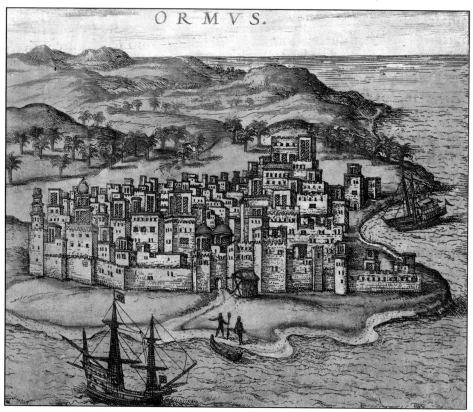

View of Hormuz city. Detail from a plate in Braun-Hogenberg's Civitates Orbis Terrarum, *Cologne 1577*

46

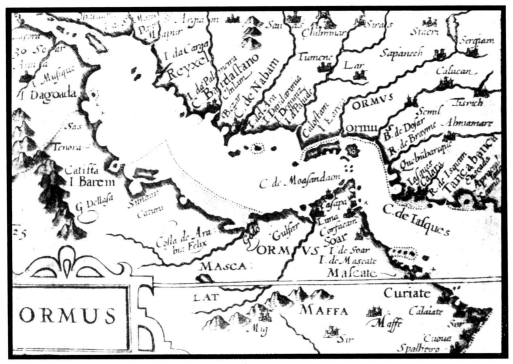

Map of 'Ormus' (Hormuz) by Petrus Bertius published in 1602

Hormuz to decide what political course to take and to build an economic power which remained unchallenged until the arrival of the Portuguese in the 16th century.

The fleet of Hormuz positioned at the entrance of the Gulf was able to take advantage of the monsoon system of the Indian Ocean and of the year-round navigation of the Gulf. To exercise their commercial monopoly the Hormuzi rulers did not require a formal political control over the neighbouring countries, but kept in the main port-towns walis in charge of collecting duties. On the Omani coast control was exsercised in Sohar, Muscat and Qalhat, while the other smaller settlements had only to follow the trade organization dictated by Hormuz in order to get some profit.

Hormuz was the centre of international contacts and reports of many travellers describe the activity of the harbour. In the 15th century there were various economic and diplomatic missions from China (in 1433 a Chinese fleet was for two months at anchor there) and all this activity did not fail to involve also Musandam.

Evidence of contemporary agricultural development and surface finds of Chinese and Hormuzi pottery witness the participation of the Musandam population in the general wealth of that period.

At the end of the 14th century Iran was invaded by the army of Timur-Lenk, Tamerlane of European historians, and Kerman was occupied in 1394, while Hormuz was left indipendent against the payment of a tribute and actually saw the volume of its trade increase in response to a growing demand from the towns of central and northern Iran.

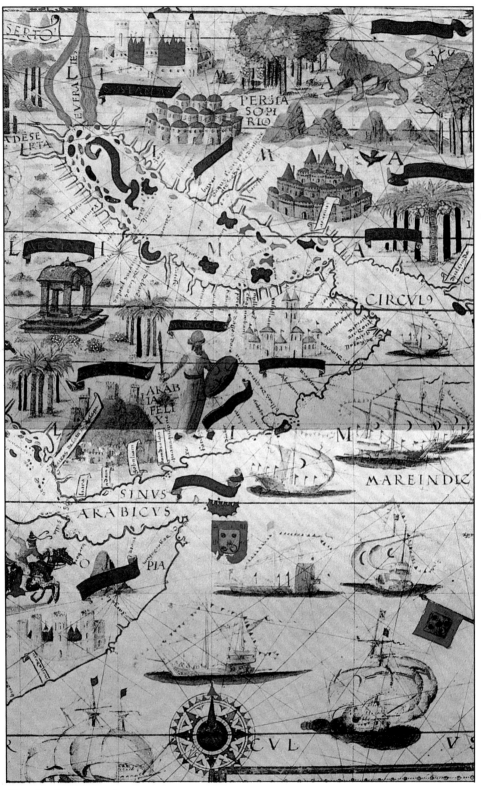

Detail of a map of Asia in the Lopo Homem-Reinel Atlas, dating from 1519

48

The Portuguese fleet before Cape Musandam battle of 1554.
From the anonymous Livro de Lizuarte de Abreu *(circa 1564)*

During the following century Hormuz was still unchallenged on the international economic scene, but at home various dynastic crises were undermining its power. Tension between Arab and Persian elements of the population and dissension among members of the ruling family reduced the kingdom to such a state of weakness that the Portuguese had no great difficulty in conquering the island (1515) which became one of the key-ports of their Empire.

The Portuguese had appeared in the Indian Ocean ready for an armed venture in 1498 when the four ships of Vasco da Gama reached Calicut. Within a few years the Portuguese *Estado da India* was established from the Cape of Good Hope to the Far East, ruled by a Governor who had his seat in Goa. The town was captured in 1510 and the advantage of its excellent position 8 km up the estuary of the Mandovi river was immediately seen. It was thus protected by sea storms and at the same time separated from the mainland by a creek. Soon a chain of 23 fortress-towns was established from the African coast to Malacca (occupied in 1511) which were to control the sea trade of the Indian Ocean.

The commercial success of the Portuguese was based mainly on the supply of spices (pepper from Sumatra, cinnamon from Ceylon, camphor from Borneo, nutmeg from Banda Islands, cloves from the Moluccas) to the European markets, and subordinately on duties imposed in the region under their control. They were also successful at promoting and taking advantage of commercial exchanges between different parts of their empire, such as imports of horses from Oman to India, and the export of Indian cottons to Africa and the East Indies.

From the fortified key-ports the Portuguese were able to impose the system of 'passes': a sort of duty that every ship had to pay for safe navigation in the Indian Ocean. In the Gulf they had other minor bases, but Hormuz was adequate to check shipping and revenues.

Portuguese tenacity in achieving their plans, and their naval gunnery provided initial supremacy in the Indian Ocean; however, such an effort could not last and towards the end of the 16th century the decay had begun. Ineptitude and corruption of officials weakened the structures from within, while shortage of ships and manpower due to the small population of Portugal, reduced the possiblity of action and the efficient patrolling of the seas.

At the beginning of the 17th century the Portuguese supremacy was challenged by local powers.

In 1622 the Persians succeeded in conquering Hormuz, while the Omanis took Julfar inflicting a serious blow, both economic and strategic. Muscat still in Portuguese hands replaced Hormuz as the main entrepot and at the same time became the base for the control of passes, but its position was soon threatened by the Omani forces united under Nasir bin Murshid who was determined to free the country from foreign occupation.

The international scene was further complicated by the appearance in the area of English and Dutch ships with the purpose of establishing their own trade.

After the conquest of Hormuz the Persians tried to press forward their success occupying Khor Fakkan and Sohar but failed to conquer Muscat, defended by Ruy Freire de Andrade. Under his vigorous leadership Sohar and Khor Fakkan changed hands again, but not Hormuz. At this juncture the possession of Musandam appeared useful: Khasab had perhaps already received some attention from the Portuguese in the 16th century; however until Hormuz kept its pre-eminent position in the chain of fortress towns there was no reason to devolop any further base in Musandam considering also that it lacked ports suitable for large ships.

In 1625 the Italian traveller Pietro della Valle, sailing back from India, recorded that not all ports on the Omani coast were safe for the Portuguese: his ship avoided in fact Diba and landed instead in Limah, the only fairly large port of the Musandam region on the Indian Ocean, to take fresh provisions. Unfortunately Pietro della Valle was kept in his cabin by a fever and could not describe the port.

After Limah his ship sailed around the Musandam cape and he reported that it was a tradition of the local sailors to greet the success of the hazardous passage with shouts of joy.

He met then Ruy Freire de Andrade on Goat Island: 'which lies near the continent Arabia almost inside a cove where there is safe anchorage for small ships'.

The fort of Khasab, perhaps already built some time around the beginning of the century, became particularly useful to the Portuguese when Ruy Freire proceded to blockade Hormuz while waiting for naval support from Goa. He was so successful in this that in 1624 the Persians were able to convince the English and Dutch fleets of giving them their support against the Portuguese.

A combined fleet reached Hormuz in December of the same year ready to fight the Portuguese and in February 1625 the Portuguese fleet under the leadership of Nuño Alvarez Botelho joined forces with Ruy Freire: the battle started 'very hot, fearce and cruel'; it lasted two days, and the casualities were enormous on both sides, but the situation was particularly difficult for the Portuguese who had dockyard facilites in Muscat only, while the Dutch and English retired to Gombroon (Bandar Abbas) for refitting and provisioning with food and ammunition.

Botelho refused to move from the area and decided to wait for the allied fleet to leave Gombroon. This happened on the 23rd of February when for various reasons Dutch and English refused to remain and help further the Persians.

When the Portuguese and allies met again 6 leagues SE of Cape Musandam, all the efforts of the allied squadron were concentrated against Botelho's flagship which put up a stiff resistance.

Both sides were short of ammunition and could not continue the engagement so that neither side gained any real advantage.

Certainly the Portuguese managed to hold their own in both actions only thanks to Nuño Alvarez Botelho whose zeal, perseverance and personal courage inspired the whole fleet. It was then decided that part of the Portuguese fleet would return to Goa, while Ruy Freire resumed the blockade, but Hormuz was not going to be retaken. A new danger was building up against the Portuguese from the interior of Oman: Imam Nasir bin Murshid had slowly united the Omani tribes and in 1633 he occupied the fort built by Ruy Freire in Julfar only three years before, and in 1644 the fort of Khasab.

The Portuguese Viceroy still hoping to change the situation in the Gulf in 1650 was giving instructions to recover Khasab, while pursuing diplomatic attempts with Persia to purchase Hormuz. Neither diplomatic manoeuvres, nor naval skirmishes were successful. Not only Hormuz was lost for ever but also in the same year 1650 Muscat, the last foothold of the Portuguese in Oman, fell into the hands of Seif bin Sultan al Ya'ariba, successor to Nasir bin Murshid.

The defeat of the Portuguese in Muscat considerably reduced their power, but did not bring back the Gulf under the sole control of the local populations.

The policy of Shah Abbas to open Iran to wider contacts, had attracted Dutch and English with the prospect of successful commercial enterprises. Both East India Companies opened a factory in Bandar Abbas (Gombroon) in 1623; in 1643 the English moved to Basra to establish another commercial base. Soon they were followed by the Dutch who seemed on the way to monopolize the commercial activity of the Gulf. Towards the second quarter of the 18th century though, the Dutch influence was very much diminished: they left Basra and the British East India Company from the residency in Bushire (established in 1778) acquired a special position and involvement in the Gulf affairs.

During the 17th and early 18th century the Ya'ariba rulers of Oman managed with a vigorous political activity to dominate the Gulf and to establish a stronger presence in East Africa, which, from a marginal position held in the oceanic trade when the main commercial route was through the Gulf, was now acquiring a more important place since all European traffic was rounding the Cape of Good Hope.

The Omani navy, in the face of Portuguese aggression, was modernized: a number of western style ships armed with modern weapons were built in Bombay. Muscat became the main port of the Gulf/Indian Ocean area and the Ya'ariba established strong positions on both sides of the Gulf, holding Bahrein and Lingah.

In the middle of the 18th century in order to save himself from family rivalries and tribal warfare the last Ya'riba ruler called on the ruler of Iran Nadir Shah for help.

Nadir Shah, ambitious and determined to extend his empire which already stretched from Iraq to Punjab to the Gulf, had started building up a fleet in Bushire and therefore welcomed the opportunity of gaining a hold on the Omani coast foreseeing future advantages. His plans were wrecked by the resistance put up by Ahmed Al Said, at the time governor of Sohar. The aspiration of Persia to dominate the Gulf were finally destroyed by the death of Nadir Shah in 1747.

While Persian influence diminished, the Qawasim coalition increased in aggressiveness. The name Qawasim used to be applied by the British authorities in Bombay to all Arabs of the Gulf coast: they were in reality a section of the Huwala tribe who had created a federation of tribes held together by mutual convenience. Their capital was Ra's al-Khaymah and their influence extended to Musandam, except for the most mountainous part of the peninsula occupied by the Shihuh.

The Qawasim rulers and the Sultan of Oman carried on a long struggle to impose their authority on the whole region. A rather tenuous Omani suzerainty was always preferred by the Shihuh, from the moment when Ahmed Al Said, having expelled the Persians from Bukha, extended his influence occupying the fort of Khasab. The Shihuh maintained a hostile attitude towards the Qawasim and disputes usually broke out between them about rights in costal markets, or about beaches where the Shihuh landed their fishing boats, particularly at Bayah and Diba where many of them lived during the summer months.

The Qawasim strength increased during the last part of the 18th century establishing some communities on Qishm and Lingah. Towards the end of the century they recognised the authority of the Wahhabis, the puritans who were expanding from the Nejd and spreading their uncompromising religious views on all the other Arab tribes from Makkah to the Gulf shores.

The attacks on local ships by the Qawasim were disturbing enough for Oman, but between 1797 and 1803 they became more frequent also against British ships trading in Bandar Abbas, so that a strong reaction by the East India Company was felt inevitable in order to re-establish peace in Gulf waters and respect for British shipping. A number of actions were mounted against the Qawasim with the support of the Sultan of Oman and in January 1820 an agreement was reached with the main sheikhs of the region who accepted a General Treaty of Peace. British vessels employed to enforce the peace terms chose Basidu on Qishm island as their naval base.

The East India Company concern in the Gulf, which had arisen out of purely commercial considerations, slowly became more political when the Company first and then the British Government took upon themselves the task of preserving peace at sea.

In the 19th century the Gulf acquired a special position not so much for commercial navigation, but because it was vital for communications between India and England, which were all the more important because of strains between European nations, as it was becoming increasingly clear to the British that not only France, but also Russia, were interested in making their presence felt in the Indian Ocean.

The system of communications changed radically when in 1840 steam navigation was introduced. The British India Steam Navigation Co. started with a mail contract first to Calcutta and Rangoon, then to Ceylon and Karachi, extending it in 1862 into the Gulf where the mail service connected Bombay, Karachi, Muscat and Basra. The opening of the Suez canal (1869) was another great step towards uniting Europe and India; at the time the most important service between the two was operated by the Peninsular and Oriental Co. founded in 1840.

The technological revolution in Europe had a particular influence on the telegraphic communications, especially in the Indian Ocean where it made possible a more direct involvement of Britain in the region.

A telegraphic land line was operating between Baghdad and Scutari in 1858,

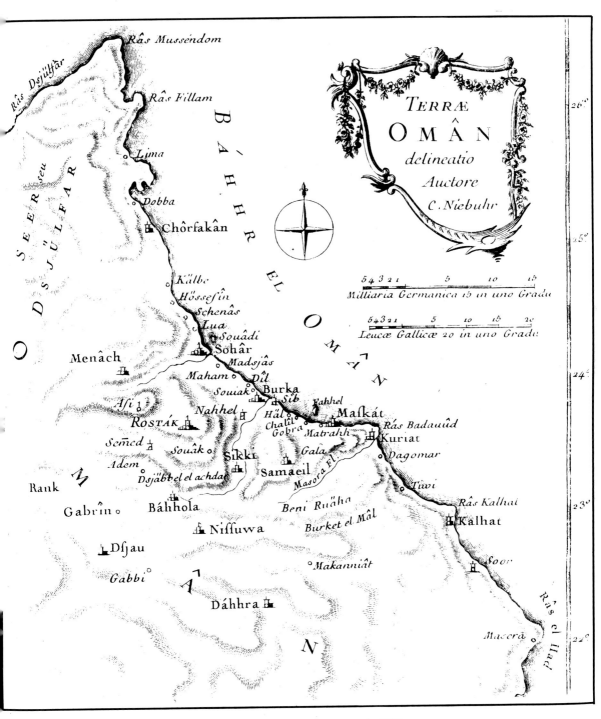

Detail from the Persian Gulf map by C. Niebuhr, Paris 1773

53

when the ambitious project of connecting to this system also India through a land line from Baghdad to Basra and a submarine cable in the Gulf, was proposed.

The project required lengthy diplomatic discussions between Turkey (under whose government Iraq was), Persia and Britain, but eventually in January 1864, after a first stretch with an aerial line was accomplished, came the most difficult part of the project which involved laying a submarine cable from Karachi to Fao.

On the 4th of February a shore-end was landed at Gwadar, on the 8th at Jask, then the expedition crossed the Gulf of Oman to land a cable on the Maqlab Isthmus which was at the shortest distance from Gwadar.

At this point difficulties with the Zahuriyn of the Maqlab Isthmus caused a month's delay. The troubles were caused by the understandable desire of the Zahuriyn of getting for themselves whatever advantage could be reaped without recognising the authority of the Sultan of Muscat with whom the British party had previously come to an agreement over the right to establish a telegraph line. In fact it appears from official records that there was some doubt over the jurisdiction of the region also in the eyes of the British authorities who since 1836 had tried to ascertain the position of the Shihuh tribes.

After discussions in Muscat, the Sultan reaffirmed his authority over Musandam, while in the meantime many of the difficulties had been settled and work could proceed: the line was taken to Elphinstone inlet and from there to a small island in the inlet itself, which was selected because it seemed to afford more security than the mainland. The island was named Telegraph islet and a station was erected and maintained there until 1869.

On March 18th the British ships moved to Bushire, then Rishahr (still on the Persian coast) and to al-Faw where the work encountered serious difficulties. Mud flats in fact kept the ships far from the shore and the cable had to be hand-dragged by men, partly swimming and partly wading. Operations were eventually completed and on April 18th 1864 telegraphic communications were officially opened between al-Faw and India.

During this part of the century the involvement of Britain in the Gulf had a lasting effect in the production of naval surveys and charts. The need for a more intimate knowledge of the south-western coastline was strongly felt and a first survey of the west coast of the Gulf, starting from Ras Musandam, was carried out after the peace treaty of 1820 with the Qawasim, to be completed in 1825. Operations were then undertaken in the Gulf of Oman and the Omani coast was surveyed between 1833 and 1837. Revisions were made in the following years and constant improvements were implemented such as establishing tidal observation stations and adding more accurate determinations of geographic co-ordinates.

At the beginning of the current century the political position of Musandam was accepted by all interested parties and the allegiance of the Musandam tribes to the Sultan of Oman was no longer disputed. In the Gulf waters British ships from the headquarters in Bushire were kept on patrol for the prevention of local hostilities and the suppression of slave trade and illegal arms traffic.

The effect of peaceful relations between France and Britain at the beginning of the century were also felt in the Indian Ocean where general peace prevailed, until the two world wars, after which British policies in the region changed, reducing direct involvement in the Gulf.

The discovery of oil in Persia in 1908 opened a new era of foreign commercial interest in the region: as well as the Europeans, the Americans arrived on the scene. The independence of India and the creation of Pakistan were also fac-

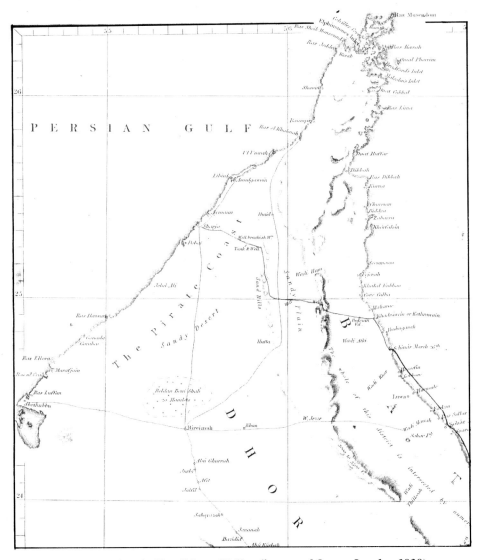

The Musandam peninsula (detail from Wellsted's map of Oman, London 1838)

tors in the changing balance of power.

All the while, life in Musandam, only briefly touched by modern technology in the 1860s' went on just above subsistence level.

The situation changed completely after 1970 when with determination and political skill His Majesty Sultan Qaboos bin Sa'id brought the whole of the Sultanate, Musandam included, to participate in the contemporary events of the region as an active partner and no longer as a silent spectator: once again the Strait of Musandam became a waterway of strategic importance.

THE ARCHITECTURE
OF THE COASTAL SETTLEMENTS

KHASAB

By local and traditional standards a town of considerable size, Khasab is the seat of the regional Governor and historically the main centre of Musandam. Its beautiful bay, at the mouth of a large wadi which extends several kilometres inland, is a fine shelter for native boats. The name Khasab may be a contraction of the two words 'khawr' (Arabic for inlet, bay) and 'Asabon', the ancient name of the promontory as mentioned by Pliny and also by the Periplus of the Erythraean Sea (para. 35)

Although the main local activity is agriculture, Khasab has a long tradition of diversified economy. The inhabitants, mostly Shihuh and Kamazirah, with a small community of Zahuriyn, are boat builders, fishermen, traders and craftsmen. In the market area a number of blacksmiths were active until recently (1980) manufacturing anchors, tools, agricultural implements and the famous small axehead (*jerz*). Khasab craftsmen are the renowned builders of the *batil*, a boat large enough to be used not only for off-shore fishing and regional trading, but also for seafaring on the Indian Ocean routes.

The extensive oasis of Khasab is based on silt deposits which appear to be of artificial origin at least in their highest levels. According to the gemorphological studies of the Royal Geographic Society expedition it is possible that exceptional floods accumulated thick deposits behind the storm beach, long before man interfered with artificial dams. Some of the dams may have been built to control flooding which sweeps the wadi floor after exceptionally long and heavy rain. Ravaging floods are known to have occurred within living memory, causing havoc. Among the priority projects of the Musandam Development Committee there are several flood control dams to be built in the lower part of Wadi Khasab. Over the lower deposits, or 'Makhus formation', after the name of the upper Wadi Khasab, the overlying alluvium shows a thickness of about 2 m. (near the coast). (Vita-Finzi, 1973:415).

A few potsherds found within this alluvium by the R.G.S. expedition were considered relatively recent (15th to 19th century A.D.) (Vita-Finzi, op.cit.:418). It seems therefore unlikely that any archaeological evidence of great antiquity can be recovered from layers higher than 3 to 2 m. below the present surface of the wadi terraces.

The first and only archaeological survey carried out in the Musandam area in 1972-73 involved merely surface collection at some thirty sites which did not include Khasab itself. At the small cove of Dib Dibba to the NE of the town, where the R.G.S. expedition base camp was established, one sherd of Sasanian decorated ware and a few fragments of 13th-14th century A.D. celadon and early and late Ming porcelain were picked up from the surface (De Cardi 1973:15-16 and App. 1). Although the town and oasis were not investigated, it is to be emphasized that no evidence of early settlement was noticed in the area. In this respect one should bear in mind that, beside the thick layer of sediments already mentioned, which would have obscured any surface trace of early occupation in the oasis, there is also to be taken into consideration the remarkable subsidence which has affected the area, combined with the post-glacial rise in the sea-level. The remains of any site which may have existed near the coast would have been submerged or destroyed.

It may be relevant to note that at low water level during spring low-tides the bay has tidal sand flats which extend for an area of about 4 square km.

The oasis and town of Khasab occupy the whole wadi floor between the two steep sides of the valley. The only gap through houses and cultivated areas are the drainage courses which are swept by violent flooding after heavy rain. The main channel is along the western side of the valley and at a short distance from it. A small re-entrant in the mountain cliff and a low terrace in front of it form the ground of the main built-up area which extends towards the sea as far as the high tide line.

Khasab. Diagram of the settlement lay-out

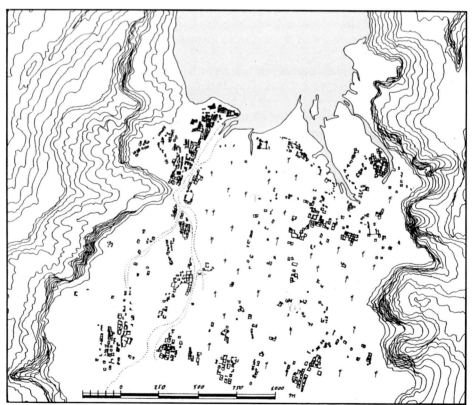

Accross the main wadi bed the oasis develops towards the eastern side of the valley being bisected by two smaller storm channels which are in fact less than a third of the main one (in width and depth). The storm channels which are dry most of the time are normally used as main north-south throughfares across the palm groves. These are interrupted at quite a few places by scattered houses. A large fortified compound surrounded by a few buildings stands at the eastern side of the main wadi drainage mouth, and at high tide its walls are often washed by the sea. The oasis extends for over 1,5 km inland and includes various fields and open areas. In one of these, about 500 m. from the shore stands the fortified compound of the Kamazirah surrounded on the northern and eastern sides by the summer dwellings of the tribe. Sur al-Kamazirah is a square stone and mud-brick enclosure, measuring 25 m. on the side with round towers at two diagonally opposite corners and a well in the centre of the courtyard. The only entrance is in the middle of the northern side. The gate is defended by inner structures; remains of few other walls are also visible around the courtyard, but everything is in a very bad state of repair.

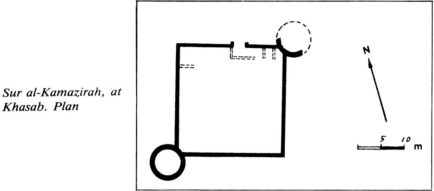

Sur al-Kamazirah, at Khasab. Plan

According to information gathered by Mr Peter Sichel (pers. comm.) the *sur* was built during the reign of Sultan Thuwaini bin Said bin Sultan (1856-1866) by two sheikhs from Kumzar: Mohammed bin Ali bin Zaydu and Mahdi bin Ali, members of the Bani Hadiyah confederation.

The temporary dwellings used by seasonal workers are nothing more than palm-frond huts, sometimes just sheds, hidden in the palm-gardens. Only the summer houses of the Kamazirah, aligned in good order near the tribe's *sur*, form a homogeneous group of buildings of very distinct character.

Each house, rectangular in plan and measuring about 7 × 3 metres, rests on six square pillars which constitute the basic skeleton of the construction and extend up to roof level.

The floor is set at about 1.5 m. from ground level and the resulting space is commonly used as a protected outdoor area. Entrance is through the only opening of the house, a door in the middle of the northern side, which is approached via a straight flight of masonry steps.

Wall panels are made of stripped palm-leaf stems held together by strings. Stems are tied together top to tail, in order to obtain an equal distribution of thickness. The spacing from stem to stem, resulting from the thickness of the string, ensures maximum air circulation and at the same time privacy. Occupants of the house can in fact look out easily whereas from the outside nothing can be seen in the darker interior.

59

Summer houses of the Kamazirah community at Khasab

In order to increase air circulation and allow better lighting a horizontal bracing is firmly tied at about 50 cm. from the top end of the panels and from that level every other group of four stems is cut and removed.

The roof is made of a double layer of complete palm-fronds, kept in position by beams and ropes. It is interesting to note that these box-houses are similar to the summer quarters which are often erected in Khasab on the top of permanent masonry buildings.

Much older is the other fort of Khasab, which is situated by the sea shore on the eastern side of the main wadi. The building incorporates the ruin of a round tower which stands awkwardly right in the middle of the courtyard: according to local tradition it is part of a fort built by the Portuguese in the 17th century.

The present building is basically a rectangular enclosure with several interrelated buildings along the northern, lower side, running parallel to the shore. The western side is very close to the bank of the wadi. On the tiny tongue of land which divides the northern side of the fort from the sea a few low buildings and a small mosque stand on a straight line bordering the high tide mark.

The building is a bewildering mixture of styles, types of masonry and materials, each from a different epoch. Wadi pebbles, random stones, carefully dressed blocks, fine plasterwork, mud-bricks, cement blocks and reinforced concrete are all visible in the construction. The oldest part appears to be the isolated round tower: an enigmatic structure in dilapidated condition which today looks totally out of context. One even wonders why the ruin, which would appear to most people as nothing but a useless and cumbersome heap of stones, has been maintained at all, standing as it does, in the middle of an important public building.

60

Helicopter view of the fort of Khasab (1980)

Whether intentional or accidental, its fortunate preservation has retained an important piece of evidence for the history of the site. As is often the case with unrestored ruins, the old tower of Khasab leaves no room to doubt that it is the oldest architectural relic visible in the area.

The tower has a maximum diameter of 7.5 m. and is preserved to a height of about 4 m.. Up to this level the tower is solid, but the remains of a sturdy spine visible in the centre are evidence of the original existence of one or two upper storeys. The complete tower, though larger in size, must have been similar in shape and proportions, to the round tower standing by the NW corner of the fort. Preserved up to the parapet of the top floor this tower is also solid in its lower part, with its raked walls standing at a height of about 6 m. from the ground. Above this level the tower has a gun room with three gun-ports evenly spaced with four groups of three arrow-slits. The wall is pierced also by an upper row of musket-holes; each hole is positioned at the centre of each interval of the lower openings. The top floor is an unroofed firing platform, protected by a parapet with arrow-slits and crenellated by small battlements. The tower is built completely with random angular stones and wadi pebbles set in thick mortar and covered by mud-render. Not long ago the upper structure has been re-rendered with a lime plaster which seems to bond weakly with the wall masonry and at various places has already fallen off. It seems likely that the tower has been built in two chronological phases. The upper structure looks very similar in style and construction, and is possibly contemporary, to the gate-tower which incorporates and defends the only entrance to the fort. This well-proportioned three-storey building is now partly obscured by an ugly construction which abutts its eastern wall. This recent addition which is adjoined on the eastern side by a second, larger

61

Khasab fort: NW tower

building has destroyed the original design of the gate-house which was impressively built in isolation above the fort entrance. Other parts of the fort and most of its walls show evidence of recent extensions, alterations and even reconstructions with imported materials.

The site of the fort and its surrounding grounds bear traces of a long and yet unclear history. Various areas and particularly the large mounds visible at foundation level by the NE and SE corners of the fort should be archaeologically investigated. The analogy of the two round towers mentioned above may suggest the possible existence of a smaller original square fort with round towers at its NW and SE corners. Without excavations, however, any suggestion of chronological phases remains merely speculative.

Recommendations have been made to restore the building and use it to house a future regional museum. If the project is going to be implemented it should include systematic archaeological excavations aimed at clarifying the history of the site.

The market of Khasab is located in the main built-up area of the town on the west bank of the wadi. The market includes some thirty shops (1979) and a few workshops which usually sell items related to their trade.

The market shops, preceded by a portico, line two streets in a T-shaped lay-out. They appear of relatively recent construction and do not offer any distinct feature worthy of mention.

At Khasab the houses are generally of good quality and have a certain degree of local character. The lay-out is comparable to the common house of the Gulf coasts: various rooms and a few two-storey buildings are arranged in a square plan around a central courtyard. The older buildings almost invariably include a wind-tower (*badjir*)

Windtowers and other types of wind catchers are common on the coasts of the Gulf, from Kuwait to Bahrain, Qatar and Dubai. Windtowers occur mainly

Windtower of Khasab

in central Persia and particularly in the region of Yazd where they are employed not only in houses but also in mosques and water reservoirs. It may therefore appear surprising that the most sophisticated examples are in fact to be found outside Iran, in Dubai. In this port and centre of Gulf trade most of the houses with wind towers are to be found in the merchant quarter of Bastakiyah, which lies on the southern side of the creek. A few windtowers can be seen also in the quarter of Deira, on the opposite side of the inlet, but they belong to isolated houses standing amidst high-rise modern buildings and therefore do not offer the tremendous visual impact of the Bastakiyah quarter, where in the late 70s some fifty towers were still standing. The quarter of Bastakiyah, the heart of the trading life of Dubai, derives its name from the town of Bastak, in SW Iran. The original inhabitants were immigrants from Bastak in the second half of the last century who left to carry on their commerce outside the heavily taxed territory of the Qajar empire. They took with them their traditional customs, building styles and techniques, including the windtower.

The quarter of Bastakiyah grew up within a limited time span (about 1895 to 1925) through the work of a small group of master-builders. This explains the remarkable unity of style of the buildings, which all appear proudly 'over-decorated' in a flamboyant style, especially on the plaster screens of the upper floor loggias and at the top of the windtowers.

To understand correctly the diffusion of architectural features, as well as other aspects of the Gulf culture, it should not be forgotten that exchanges and contacts between the two shores of the Gulf have been always close and perhaps more frequent and easy than they were between the southern coast of Iran and the country's interior.

From time immemorial the coasts of the Gulf have been inhabited by a mixed Arab-Persian population which also included large communities of Baluchis, Indians and east Africans. The largest settlements had a very cosmopolitan style of life, which influenced all aspects of the local culture and hence the building methods.

The average traditional house of Khasab belongs to the 'Gulf type' in its simplest form and it is perhaps the utter simplicity that makes the building attractive and pleasant. The only outstanding feature is the windtower which is designed to catch one or more of the prevailing winds. The windtower can have two or more vents-cum-shafts. This system of ventilation requires an opening which catches and funnels air from the unrestricted upper levels down to the house through a vertical shaft. The tower contains a second shaft which allows inverse air-circulation: the double shaft system gives moderate ventilation even in the total absence of wind. Depending on the strength of breeze and the variations in inside and outside air temperature, as well as certain other factors (size of room, design and position of doors and windows) the ventilation created by the *badjir* can be most effective; however it is confined to the one room in the house where all the members of the family tend to concentrate during the heat of the summer.

In urban areas air movement is inhibited by the density of the buildings. In order to work effectively the *badjir* must therefore be set at a certain height above the roof-tops: in two-storey buildings it may rise at least 15 m. above ground. At that height wind velocity is about one and a half times greater than at ground level.

At Khasab many rural buildings standing in isolation amidst the trees of the oasis employ windtowers which are not higher than the top of the house. If the tower abuts other parts of the house it is obviously built to catch only the breeze blowing in one direction where the structure is on the contrary free-standing, the double shaft system allows for air blowing alternately from two opposite directions to be caught, as happens in coastal areas when the on-shore/off-shore breeze changes.

Multi-directional windtowers, open on four-sides do exist in Khasab: they contain four to six vertical shafts which may terminate at the top with three to six vents.

The thin vertical structures of the towers are strengthened by wooden tie-beams which do not obstruct air movement. The beams are also used as scaffolding for the frequent repairs, re-rendering and seasonal cleaning of the shafts, which become heavily covered in bird-droppings.

Internal structure of a large windtower at Khasab

In winter, when additional ventilation becomes unconfortable, the shafts are blocked off by wooden planks. Cloth *badjir* which are erected at the beginning of the hot season and taken down in winter were once very common on the coasts of northern Oman and were reported to have existed in Khasab, but they are no longer to be seen.

Since the introduction of electricity windtowers have sharply declined in importance. Most of the old structures have fallen into complete disuse and new ones are no longer built. Even when disused the masonry towers tend to be preserved and repaired as parts of the house, but cloth *badjir* are simply discarded and destroyed.

General view of Bukha, looking E. On the left the white tower of the main fort dominates the bay. The tower of the inland fort stands on the hill on the right, behind the white minaret of a new mosque

BUKHA

Bukha is the only large settlement belonging to Oman located on the western coast of the peninsula. Attractively situated on a crescent-shaped bay and with a relatively wide hinterland, Bukha has the physical setting of a major town, yet for a number of reasons has never developed to its maximum potential; rather, in recent times, it has dwindled to the size of a small village.

Paradoxically it has been the oil boom in the neighbouring Emirates which has accelerated the economic decline of Bukha: gradually abandoned by most of its inhabitants it has become a ghost town. The new policies of the Sultanate of Oman have inspired and supported plans for development which will hopefully revitalize Bukha and start a new period of prosperity. Good communications are of course of primary importance to create new opportunities, bring back those who have left and perhaps even attract some new people.

A small jetty has been built near the western cape and Bukha is now on the motor road to Khasab. Capital investment may make new labour available and create interest and opportunity to cultivate the old fields again, improve the water supply and renovate the dying palm groves: with the adjoining village of Jadi, Bukha may witness new growth in the exploitation of its agricultural resources and regain and even surpass the level of local farming in the past.

The settlement is divided in two densely clustered groups of houses, both very close to the water: the larger Harat al-Sharqiyah (or Eastern quarter) is situated at the centre of the bay and includes a few large buildings and a fort. A few hundred metres to the west lies Harat al-Gharbiyah (or the Western Quarter). A second fort with a tall circular tower stands on the top of a rocky hill projecting in to the middle of the plain. Further east the hinterland is formed by two small valleys with gardens and fields and isolated homesteads.

The original Shihi population, all belonging to the Bani Hadiyah, was increased not later than the end of last century by a large number of immigrants of Iranian origin. According to information collected by Lorimer at the beginning of this century Bukha had 200 houses and the inhabitants were three-fourth Iranians and one-fourth Shihuh. However, judging from the inaccurate description

New development at Bukha with the coastal road under constuction. The view is taken from the top of the fort (1979)

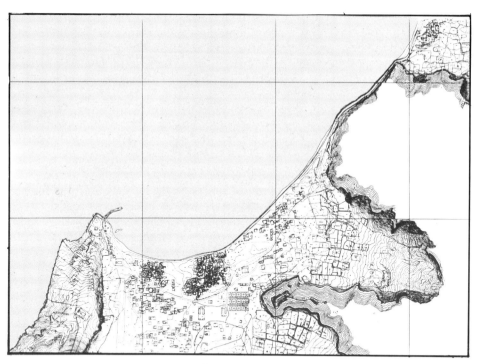

Bukha. Diagram of the settlement lay-out

of the village (only one 'square fort on a hillock' is reported and there is no mention of the second fort by the seashore and of the adjacent Great Mosque) Lorimer's information on Bukha is to be considered unreliable.

The original population seems in fact to have settled in the area of the Harat al-Sharqiyah which was protected by a fort, perhaps of the *sur* type and in the course of time became constricted on the eastern and western sides by extensive graveyards. When newcomers were allowed to settle in the area they could use the existing large Friday Mosque, but were prevented from joining the built-up area by the presence on either side of the quarter of the vast burial grounds.

The layout of both quarters is rather irregular but in the eastern one the development pattern appears guided and formalised by two factors: first by the existence of large public buildings, like the fort and the Great Mosque and secondly by the growth of two rows of prominent houses at the eastern and northern end of the built-up area. The northern line of buildings, overlooking the beach (and now the new corniche road) comprises a few two-storey houses, including the house of the sheikh.

The fort of Bukha is a stone building, square in plan, with rectangular towers at the SE and NW corners and a round tower at the SW corner.

Originally standing right on the shore, it was surrounded on three sides by a shallow moat filled with sea water. In the middle of the northern side a square salient frames the only entrance to the fort: a narrow gateway with a pointed false arch, coarsely formed by oversailing courses of stones. The door is set slightly recessed from the outer wall, leaving a gap above the entrance: it is a defensive device known as *kuwwa* or *maskat*: ubiquitous in Oman in all fortified buildings, the *kuwwa* allows defenders to pour water on any fire lit by attackers to burn down the door.

68

The beach fort of Bukha, looking NW. In the foreground the vast eastern cemetery .

Plan of the eastern quarter of Bukha with outlined major buildings, based on a 1:1000 scale map

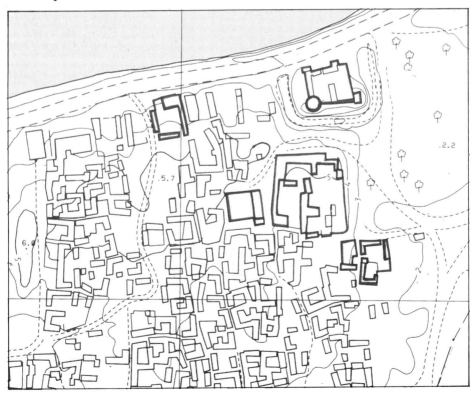

70

The most outstanding feature of the fort is undoubtedly the tall, round tower at the SW corner. Its plan is circular, but the external walls, pierced by two rows of arrow slits and a lower row of four cannon ports, gradually curve inwards, to reach a much smaller diametre near the top where the last courses of the crenellated parapet rise almost cylindrically.

The curious tower which could be described as pear-shaped may be seen as the casual result of the builders' attempt to reach a pronounced tapering of the walls within a relatively limited height. The perfect symmetry of the construction and the accuracy of the stonework are instead proof of an intentional and refined design. The combination of horizontal and vertical curving of the walls is in fact most effective to reduce the impact of cannon balls. The tower displays undoubtedly a unique design, and it has become an unmistakable landmark in the area.

The structure bears traces of restoration which may date to various epochs. The original construction seems to include the gun-ports and cannot therefore be earlier than the 16th century A.D. The fort is since long disused and, apart from the towers, which are rather well preserved, the rest of the building is very dilapidated and partly roofless. Many rooms however show traces of better days in the remains of rich wall decoration and carved doors and shutters.

The eastern quarter of Bukha looking S from the fort walls. The Great Mosque stands in the centre

Beach fort at Bukha, the gate (facing page)

Beach fort at Bukha, the SW tower, looking NE (facing page)

Not far from the fort stands the second most important building of Bukha: the Great Mosque.

With its high walls rising from a rectangular terrace measuring 27 × 22m the mosque towers above the small houses of the quarter.

On the south side a double staircase gives access to the ablution area from where two doors open on the mosque courtyard. On the opposite side similar steps lead directly to the forecourt.

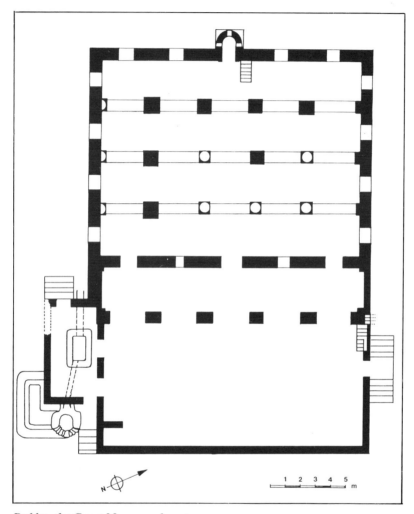

Bukha, the Great Mosque, plan

The mosque proper is formed by four aisles parallel to the *qibla* wall and is preceded by one aisle porch open onto the forecourt. A flat roof supported by high pillars covers hall and portico. Parallel to the *qibla* wall the intercolumnia in the prayer hall are spanned by pointed arches. These have a limited static function and are mainly decorative: they are formed by rubble masonry encased by gypsum tiles delicately decorated by mould-cast patterns. The basic motifs are alternating rows of arches and rosettes. The *mihrab* is a plain niche with three small square windows open almost at floor level. No decoration frames the niche on the inside.

72

Bukha, the Great Mosque.
Interior, looking SW

Bukha, the Great Mosque.
Detail of the cast stucco decoration

73

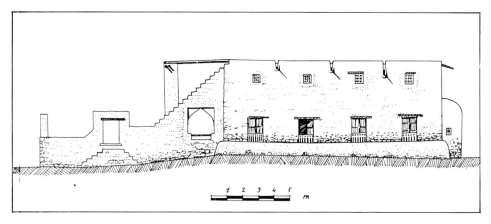

Bukha the Great Mosque. North elevation

Bukha, the Great Mosque. Detail of qibli *wall, showing window grills and* mihrab *salient*

Only a very crude wooden *minbar* was found inside the mosque: perhaps a cheap copy of a lost original which may have rested on a few masonry steps still visible beside the *mihrab*.

On the whole the outer walls of the mosque are bare and the stonework is finished by a thin lime and mud render; decoration is confined to the window plaster grills. They display a great variety of motifs, from purely geometric to plant and foliate patterns. The carving is not refined but crisp and lively and due to the good quality *saruj* plaster, the design is followed to the most delicate details. The strong contrast between the dark background and the light surface of the tracery makes the thinnest points of contact almost unnoticeable giving the grille the delicate and light appearance of lacework.

The average house of Bukha recalls the common courtyard type of the Gulf area in its simplest form. There are no wind-towers and no terraced roofs. The

Bukha, a street of the eastern quarter

main living area is the courtyard where privacy is ensured by various one-storey rooms sited along the high boundary walls. These rooms all look inwards except the *majlis*, a sitting/guest room which usually has windows and the main entrance overlooking the street. In most cases this room is adjoined by washing facilities and a lavatory. The external walls of the houses have otherwise no windows at all: this creates a very special atmosphere in the narrow streets and alleys of the town, lined by bare and mud plastered walls. The family rooms overlooking the courtyard are used both for living and sleeping and often have an 'internal' washing area, separated from the rest of the room by a low crenellated partition wall.

A less common type of house has a portico running in front of the main wing of the building, overlooking the courtyard. In some cases as in the large sheikhly house of Harat al-Sharqiyah, the building develops on two storeys, both with porticos: the massive framework of the house extends to the front of the building where the structures remain exposed and visible.

Bukha, main wing of the Sheikh's residence

KUMZAR

Kumzar is tucked into Khor Kumzar, a large bight preceded by two islands and situated right in the middle of the Peninsula's northern headlands.

It is an amazing place where every single aspect is an extreme and can be expressed only by a superlative.

It is the northernmost settlement of the Sultanate, the most densely populated, the village with the largest number of boats in relation to the population, the smallest number of dogs, the shortest length of roads and the smallest number of trees. Kumzar has also the smallest number of tribal groups: there are only Kamazirah there.

Approaching Kumzar from the sea

To say that its houses are closely packed is an understatement: they literally fill the tiny, narrow valley, called Wadi Marwan, from side to side wherever possible. The only gap through the mass of closely crowded houses is a narrow wadi channel which is the drainage for the entire valley.

The village has two mosques, now restored and partly rebuilt with the addition of a minaret. The two mosques stand close together near the shore and are surrounded by two small graveyards described by Bertram Thomas as 'full to overflowing long centuries ago'. Lack of burial ground is perhaps the only reason for the practice of burying 'their dead in their own houses under their living rooms' as reported with some perplexity by the same author.

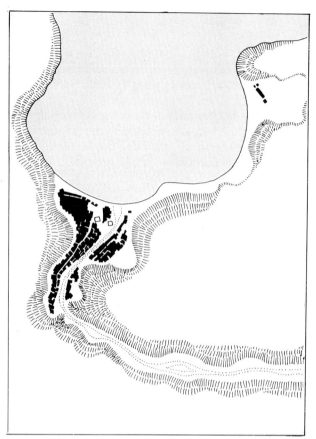

Kumzar. Sketch-map of the settlement lay-out

Kumzar. A view of the town along Wadi Marwan, with Khor Kumzar visible in the background

Before the recent construction by the Government of a desalination plant, water could only be obtained from a large and copious well at the back of the village.

According to Lorimer, at the beginning of this century there were 600 houses at Kumzar and 40 or 50 fishing boats. It seems interesting to compare the number of houses to the 300 of Khasab and 200 of Bukha, reported by the same author. According to Thomas at his time Kumzar had about a 'hundred fishing *batils* dismasted and drawn up with singular uniformity along the yellow sandy beach'. Judging from the length of the beach one cannot refrain from thinking that the 'singular uniformity' of the beached boats was simply due to the extreme lack of space. Lack of space is also why movement along the village is mainly through the wadi bed (which is obviously dry most of the time) and one single narrow street linking the main mosque to the sheikh's house and the upper wadi. The stone houses built with tiny courtyards and without terraced roofs, leave very little space for pedestrian movement and even the main thoroughfare narrows at places to less than a metre.

The appearance of the houses of Kumzar does not mitigate in any measure the gloom of the site, which is shut in on three sides by bare and precipitous mountains. The only place where the sombre atmosphere is somewhat relieved is along the wadi where the life of the village expands in the open and one can see fishermen repairing their nets, women working and children playing. Ledges and terraces overlooking the wadi offer here the opportunity for a certain articulation of the house form and primitive balconies and verandahs line the front of the dwellings.

The main activity of the inhabitants of Kumzar is fishing, but they also own part of the date groves of Khasab and Diba, where one of their sheikhs resides.

Kumzar, graveyard and mosque. Note domed tomb

The Kamazirah also own a considerable number of sheep and goats. Due to limited pasture available in the hinterland of the village, the animals are periodically taken by boat to graze on various grounds along the coasts and especially on Jazirat al-Ghanim, the island known in English as Goat Island, which takes its Arabic name from the flocks which have been for centuries its only seasonal occupants.

A peculiar sight, entering Kumzar bay, are the ship names painted on the rocks: a curious practice of visiting crews which echoes, although on smaller scale, the examples of Jazirat al-Ghanim and Muscat.

Kumzar, the main street

Kumzar, beach with a row of batil

The impressive bow of a Kumzari batil. The zoomorphic stem-piece is covered by a goat skin and decorated by strings of cowrie shells. The 'horned' bar function is to secure parts of the rigging

Kumzari batil. *The high stem is decorated with truncated cowrie shells stitched on leather straps*

Kumzar harbour with painted ships' names

82

The large bay of Khasab before 1983. The town was accessible only by air or sea

The village of Hanah before the construction of the coastal road

Hanah. A few houses, a mosque and a cemetery occupy the available ground, constricted between sea and mountain

Qida. The small valley of Qida is one of the richest in vegetation including date palms and many fruit trees

The new motor road follows the rugged coastline, connecting Khasab to Ra's al-Khaymah and the northern Oman territory

The houses of Qida line the narrow valley between the cultivations and the sheer mountain side (T. Eigeland)

Untouched by the recent road development the shrine of Sheikh Masud still lies in splendid isolation between barren mountains and sea

Sand flats of Khasab bay at low tide

Helicopter view of the fort of Khasab. The site includes buildings of various epochs and betrays a remarkable archaeological potential. The buildings on the right are aligned on the high-tide mark

Khasab. House of the western quarter topped by a huge, four-side wind tower. In the foreground the wadi bed, which is occasionally swept by ravaging floods

Khasab.Small two-side wind tower of a suburban house

Bukha. Helicopter view of the eastern quarter of the town. Amidst the residential buildings stand out in the centre the Great Mosque and near the sea shore the large fort surrounded by a moat

The crenellated walls of the fort of Bukha with the massive and curiously shaped south-west tower

The bay of Bukha with the new corniche road under construction

Bukha. The Shaikh's house lifts its walls and attractive loggia above the common one-storey buildings of the town

Oblique aerial view of Kumzar (1981). Note in the centre the large house with inner courtyard by the main street and the fishing boats aligned on the beach. To the far left is the government desalination plant. (Courtesy of R.K. Vincent jr.)

Kumzar harbour

92

Batil *aligned on the tiny beach of Kumzar. The rudders are removed to facilitate beaching. With their zoomorphic sterns and shell-decorated stitched bows, the boats of Kumzar are unique among the Gulf vessels*

THE ARCHITECTURE
OF THE MOUNTAIN SETTLEMENTS

Small sites with one or two homesteads at the edge of a small field area are a common pattern of settlement in the Musandam mountains, but the average village is a hamlet of 10 to 15 houses (*bulaydah*) inhabited by an extended family. Larger villages of 20 to 50 houses (*harah*) inhabited by several families do exist, but are a minority. Most of the largest settlements have in fact witnessed a development related to factors which are external to traditional socio-economic organization. Harf Qabbi, an outstanding example of this type of expansion will be examined below.

In general, the mountain villages, all inhabited by Shihuh, have the following common characters:
— their location is next to areas of agriculture potential and where the topography permits affective control of run-off during winter rains for water storage and direct irrigation of fields;
— the setting of the village is preferably on the top of the ridges or against mountain slopes;
— dwelling units are scattered far apart from one another and their setting is dictated by the topography of the site. Areas of soft ground are required for construction;
— fortifications are normally absent: the total isolation of the settlements located in a harsh environment far from the coast and from any major track being a defence in itself;
— building materials are exclusively local.

The general settlement patterns summarized above create a very uniform type of architecture both in the house form and in the spatial organisation. Some variations however do occur due to the history of each settlement, the peculiar aspects of the socio-economic organization of its inhabitants, influence from the environment and other factors.

The examples of mountain settlement examined below have been chosen with the aim of highlighting the most typical aspects of the vernacular architecture.

As already discussed earlier, the *takhwil* or seasonal migration dictates a very original house-form in the area. During the summer from June to September, when scarcity of water makes life difficult if not totally impossible, the Shihuh move from their mountain villages to the coastal areas where hands are

The seasonal mountain hamlet of Taqada

Permanent dwellings in the upper wadi Shariyah

The large bulaydah *of Rabi'a; the village includes some permanent houses of recent construction*

The abondoned settlement of Sellian, one of the few fortified hamlets in the hinterland of Khasab

required for tending the gardens and the date harvest. The mountain villages are thus abandoned, although a few people remain behind to look after the flocks. The herdsmen take the animals to grazing grounds and waterholes hidden in remote areas of the mountains, leaving the lower wadis where the temperature becomes intolerable. The long abandonment of the villages is the reason for the construction of the very original building known as *bayt al-qufl*. Built partly underground, *bayt al-qufl* is the most important part of the house conceived and executed to achieve maximum strength for the safe preservation of the most valuable belongings of the family.

The building is in fact virtually impregnable. Rectangular in plan it has an average size of 7×4m. The walls are built of selected blocks of local stone used

A typical bayt al-qufl *of mountains (note hat by the entrance for scale)*

in their natural shape or after minimal cutting. Foundations are set at least one and half metre below ground and the walls rise about one to one and half metre above it. The roof is made of stone slabs and a thick layer of earth supported by acacia tree trunks just stripped of their bark and set accross the short side of the room. In some cases a fully stone roof is laid on cantilivered slabs. Entrance is through a small door in the middle of one long side. It is the only opening in the building and it can be shut by a heavy wooden door which extends down to the sunken floor and pivots on a stone socket. The door has two locks generally positioned as follows: the *qufl* near the top and the *zalq* in the lower part.

The *qufl* consits of two elements: the *alaq*, a piece of wood about 38 cm long, 3 cm wide and 3 cm deep in the centre, with about 16 indentations along one side. The *alaq* is a bolt which slots into a wooden housing, *bayt al-alaq*. The *alaq* is moved by manipulating a sort of key, the *malaqa*, a 30 cm lomg curved and pointed iron arm with a transverse handle at the end. The *malaqa* is inserted

Roofless bayt al-qufl *showing details of masonry. Note cantilevered slabs to support roof elements (50 cm scale)*

Ruined bayt al-qufl *showing sunken type of construction. Entrance is by the standing girl. A wall niche is visible on the short side of the room.*

thorugh a small hole in the door above the lock and manouvred into one of the indentations through a small opening in the side of the *bayt al-alaq*: The *malaqa* moves the *alaq* to the right and is then placed into the next indentation. This process is continued until the *alaq* is completely drawn back.

The *zalq* is a heavy wooden bolt partly hollow which can slide horizontally inside a vertical housing. The *zalq* is kept in the locked position by two strong pins contained in the lock housing and allowed to drop down into two holes drilled in the *zalq*.

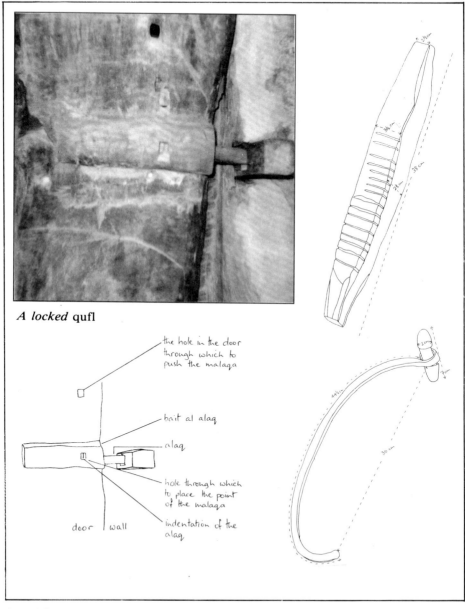

A *locked* qufl

the hole in the door through which to push the malaqa

bait al alaq

alaq

hole through which to place the point of the malaqa

indentation of the alaq

door | wall

Simplified drawing of the qufl *showing locking system from inside the room and details of* alaq *and* malaqa

100

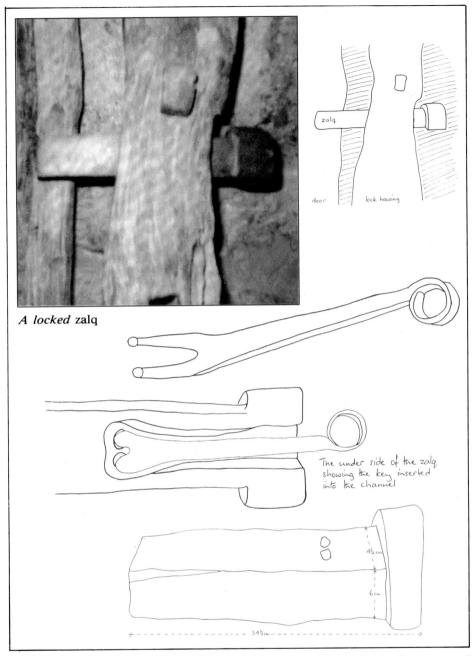

A locked zalq

The under side of the zalq showing the key inserted into the channel

4½cm

6cm

34½cm

Simplified drawing of the zalq, *showing locking system from inside the room and details of the* zalq, *key and key in position*

To release the *zalq* the opener has to stretch his hand through a hole in the wall and take hold of a suspended stick to which a key is attached. The key is then inserted into the channel inside the *zalq* and its double pointed end is pushed up into the two vertical holes where the pins have dropped, forcing them up into the lock housing. The *zalq* is now released, it can be slid back and the door is unlocked.

Door with locking knob (axe handle 85 cm long)

Deeply recessed door of a typical bayt al-qufl

Beside the two locks the door may also have a latch lock which can be rotated from outside by means of a large knob. This is used as a temporary locking device when the village is inhabited and the door remains shut only to keep goats and perhaps small children out.

Bayt al-qufl however is not only protected by the strength of the door and the two locks, but also by the design of the entrance itself. The door is usually placed at the end of an opening in the wall which is no larger than 60 × 80 cm but is over 1 m deep: the narrow passage would greatly limit any attempt to force the door open and in fact makes going in and out difficult even for the house owner.

As an example of the typical mountain dwelling a house complex of the village of Rubi was surveyed.

Rubi is a *bulaydah* of 12 houses located 7 km south of Khasab on a low mountain spur between Wadi Khasab and the short Wadi Rubi. The foot of the hill is surrounded by walled fields which stretch for a total of about one hectar on the west bank of Wadi Khasab and the south bank of Wadi Rubi. The field area is divided into several plots terraced on various levels. As is always the case in the Musandam mountains, fields are cultivated only during the short rainy season, i.e. December to January. The crops, mainly wheat and barley, depend on an extremely erratic rainfall and the Shihuh make all possible efforts to collect as much as possible from the run-off caused by the steep, impermeable hillslopes.

The water is deflected by low oblique stone walls (*masaylah*) and channelled to the uppermost plots. All fields are carefully leveled and walled in to keep goats and other animals out, prevent erosion and trap the silt. The channelled water enters the enclosures through special inlets barred by stones or wooden bars and branches. Water is then distributed along the top of the field across the surface and then allowed to flow to the lower plots through appropriate spillways.

103

Houses of the seasonal village of Rubi, overlooking Wadi Khasab. Note on the left the numerous openings of a saffah *wall*

Barred inlet to channel water into walled field

*Water deflecting wall (*musaylah*). Note channel section built on arches to span a small gully*

During the rainy season drinking water is collected in underground cisterns. The largest cisterns are located along the main wadis, but smaller tanks are also to be found near the houses. With the water-supply network presently run by the Government most of the old water gathering systems tend to be abandoned but quite a few like Birkat al-Nuss in Wadi Makhus and the large Birkat al-Khalidiyah at Sal al-A'la have been restored and kept in use. At the last site also the catchment system has been recently improved and the *masaylah* has been lined with waterproof cement.

Birka al-Khalidiyah, a large water reservoir at Sal al-A'la, recently restored

Conservation of water is obviously an essential element of fortified sites: an outstanding example is the domed cistern adjoining the tower of the hillfort of Bukha.

In his study of the Shihuh of northern Oman Walter Dostal has rightly emphasized the important practice of the *kher* (*khayr*) in relation to the problem of water shortage in the mountains. The *khayr* is a large water jar donated by an individual or a family for public use: the donor also pays for the periodical replenishment of the jar which is generally located under a tree along a main track or among the village houses. The *khayr* is a pious gesture which increases the social prestige of the donor; a custom comparable to the *sabil* of other parts of Arabia and especially of the Yemen, or in Oman to the construction of a *falaj* or a well with adjoining cistern called *waqbah*.

At Rubi there are several *khayr* jars among the houses: when the village is abandoned as it was at the time of our survey, the jar tops are protected by thorn branches.

Domed cistern within the Bukha hillfort

Khayr *jar at Rubi. Note thorn branches used as stopper when the jar is not in use*

The houses at Rubi are spread around and on the top of a low rocky hill whose natural features have been used to accommodate the various parts of the dwellings.

The living unit (house) chosen for our survey is at the south end of the village, a few metres lower than the hilltop: it consists of three buildings and several terraced interrelated areas.

The house is approached via a steep path which climbs from the fields up to a well-built retaining wall abutting a huge rock. Four steps lead onto a gravelled terrace 6 m long and 2 m wide. From these a second flight of steps, set at right angles to the first, gives access to a much larger, irregularly shaped ground. This is the house courtyard, the main living area for the whole family and the centre of the functions of the various buildings which form the house. Opposite the

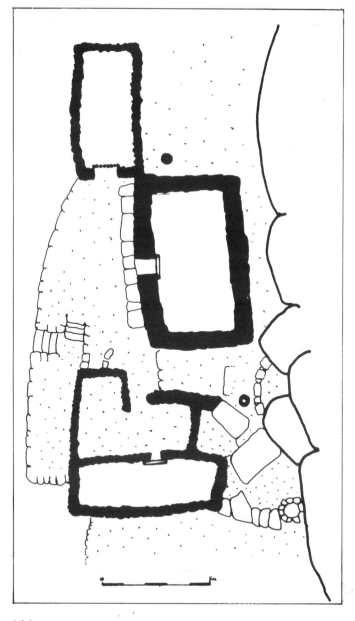

Dwelling complex at Rubi: plan

stairs is a small, roofed room built with several square apertures on the outer side and a large entrance on the courtyard. This cool and ventilated room (*saffah*) is used as a sitting area during the hot months and to keep perishable provisions like fodder and fresh vegetables. The door is closed by a hinged panel made of palm-leaf stems. The *saffah* may also occur in the form of a much simpler shed, completely open on the front, and sometimes also on the opposite side. It is not unusual for the roof of the *saffah* to be only a light palm-frond panel which can be removed in winter or when the house is unoccupied. At the vilages of Limhas and al-Hawth (Sal al-A'la) a few examples of unroofed *saffah* were noticed (winter 1982): in most cases the *saffah* was defined only by a wall with square openings at various levels, standing like a screen in front of part of the facade of the house.

Approach from the wadi to house 'A' at Rubi

Rubi, house 'A': smaller roofed room viewed from above. In the background a small area of the village fields can be seen, with a modern water tank provided by the Government (near car)

Passage between the animal pen and the bayt al-qufl. *The area is partly roofed and leads up to a washing and cooking yard*

Above the first landing and to the right of the upper staircase in the Rubi dwelling is a roofed room measuring 7×3 m preceded by a small walled yard which is used as animal pen. Against the pen enclosure is a small fireplace used almost exclusively to prepare coffee and to cook food for visitors.

On the west side of the courtyard is a *bayt al-qufl* of 8×5 m. This building rises about 1.2 m above ground and is built with very large squared blocks mixed with smaller angular stones. Along most of the front side runs a low bench of large blocks which form a kind of plinth to the building. This bench (*dekka*) is a typical feature of the mountain architecture and defines the most important space in the Shihi dwelling.

Between the animal pen and the large *bayt al-qufl* the house of Rubi extends into various small areas used for washing, cooking and storage. The washing areas are defined by large jars, one in the corner on the back of the *saffah* and the *bayt al-qufl*, and one set by a small walled space between two rocks. The cooking area ends with a large underground oven framed at ground level by a ring of stone blocks.

The house complex of Rubi shows an integrated use of various components in a spatial organization which includes both roofed and open areas. For a complete understanding of the local concept of the house and its functions, the fact should be borne in mind that rooftops are used as additional terraces. Most of the time people live and sleep in the open and enjoy the commanding view over the fields and up the wadi, to the bay of Khasab and the sea. Only during the coolest winter nights do people sleep indoors perhaps seeking the warmth of a fire burning in the hearth of *bayt al-qufl* where a truncated pot is set in the roof to let the smoke out.

Rubi, house 'A' complex: roof-top level plan

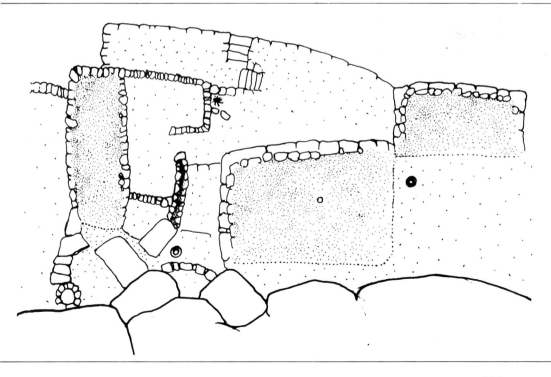

Rubi, house 'A': roof of bayt al-qufl. *The light roof of the* saffah *is visible at top right*

At the time of our visit (June 1981) the village was already deserted. It was therefore impossible for us to survey and photograph the interior of the houses.

The interior of an average *bayt al-qufl* is here illustrated by photographs of a building in the village of Limhas (Sāl al-A'la). The photos illustrate both sides of the room taken from the same central position by the door.

The floor is about 1 m below the outer threshold level, slightly higher is a large platform at each end of the room. They are linked on the side opposite the entrance by a narrow bench. The wooden door visible to the right of the first photograph pivots on a large block of stone which together with a second parallel block forms a wide step into the room. The bench and most of the platform are occupied by large storage jars which are cemented together and against the wall. The jar mouths are closed by smaller pots or wooden stoppers. The rounded bottom of the pots fits conveniently into the mouth of virtually any size of jar. To ensure an effective protection of the contents against any animal or insect the pots are made heavier by a fill of pebbles or alternatively they are tied by strings. Utensils like ropes, mats, coffee pots and bags hang from the walls of the room or from hooks tied to the ceiling.

The basic roof structure consists of large tree trunks, mostly varieties of acacia spanning the room on its shorter side. The beams, spaced less than 30 cm apart support a layer of stone slabs which are in turn overlain by a thick layer of earth. On the outside the roof is framed by a row of large, heavy slabs set on the outer walls. These slabs have the principal function of retaining the mass of loose soil which forms the top roof layer.

112

Projecting for about 20 cm from the wall face, the slabs form an attractive cornice to the building; in some cases the feature may develop to the size of a wide ledge which visually balances the *dekka* and to a certain degree protects it.

The houses of Limhas are built on low artificial terraces along the banks of the wadi, just above the highest flood level. Because of the peculiarity of its location and habitat the site is never totally abandoned all the year round. Easy communications with Khasab allow fast movements to and from the coast and

Sal al-A'la, interior of a bayt al-qufl: *area to the right of the entrance. Part of the door is visible at the extreme right*

113

even at the time of the date harvest a number of people tend to return to the village quite frequently. It is interesting to note that Wadi Khasab and Sal al-A'la in particular are the only places in northern Musandam where camels have been used until recently.

Sal al-A'la is at the head of the main valley of the largest drainage system of the Musandam mounatins which flows into the sea at Khasab. As the first component of the place name indicates it is a silt flat (*sal*) which occupies most of

Sal al-A'la, interior of a bayt al-qufl: *area to the left of entrance. Note biconical pots used as large jar stoppers*

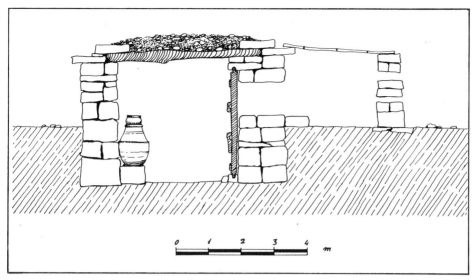

Diagram showing cross-section of typical bayt al-qufl, *with* saffah *on the right*

the large bowl surrounded on three sides by steep mountains: to the east these form only a narrow barrier separating the valley from the Gulf of Oman waters. The toponym couples the site to the neighbouring Sal al-Asfal (sometimes incorrectly spelt Sayl al-Asfal) or the lower *sal* in counterposition to the higher (al-A'la). For an area of about 35 hectares the silt plain is covered by the thickest concentration of trees to be found not only in Musandam but in northern Oman. *Acacia tortilis (samr)* and *Ziziphus spina-christi (sidr)* can reach a height of 8-9 m. Except in the hottest months the ground is covered by thick, healthy grass and the bowl is indeed a scenery of great beauty.

At the edge of the silt plain there is a small cultivation of date palms, fruit trees and other crops. The garden is encompassed by a wall which is worthy of detailed examination.

The wall is about 1.5 m high, topped by a thick crown of thorn branches. The masonry is made of random wadi pebbles and larger boulders laid dry. The sides of the enclosure parallel to the flood course and facing the lower wadi are made of selected small pebbles except for the top where a course of large boulders is laid to keep the branches in position. The other two sides of the enclosure display a more complex type of masonry: on a footing of selected flat stones the wall is made of small pebbles to a height of 60 cm. At that level large boulders are set vertically at regularly spaced intervals in order to create a row of openings. These are lightly screened by small stones or brushwood and are linteled by large slabs or oblong boulders. The upper section of the wall is made of very large boulders which by means of their sheer weight strengthen the lower structure. This peculiar type of masonry which seems to reverse the physical principle that heavier stones must be at the bottom, is in fact a skilful response to the environment: to obtain an enclosure able to withstand strong winds and heavy floodings the local builders have developed a masonry of varying texture which offers limited obstruction to the tremendous thrust of the water and great resistance at the top of the structure.

115

House of Limhas (Sal al-A'la)

Welled date garden at Sal al-A'la
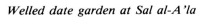

Welled date garden at Sal al-A'la: detail of upstream wall

Several groups of ruined buildings scattered in various parts of the Sal al-A'la bowl suggest a long occupation and a building tradition of ancient origin. On the occasion of the R.G.S. reconnaissance the ruins were examined by B.De Cardi who sketched a few plans and made a surface collection of artefacts. According to Miss de Cardi the oldest diagnostic material recovered were a few fragments of pottery datable to the 15th century A.D. but a high percentage in the collection was formed of undatable, plain and coarse utility wares.

At the neighbouring site of Sal al-Asfal on the other hand the collected sherds included celadon, stonewares and glazed and painted pottery datable to the 11th-14th century. From this kind of limited sampling it seems reasonable to deduce that the area bears traces of a long history of settlement (De Cardi 1975: 48-50).

The ruins visible at both sites show good quality masonry and widespread use of large ashlar blocks beside the occurrence of circular buildings and the total absence of 'sunken' houses. It should however be noted that different building types are also visible at the inhabited hamlets of Sal al-A'la where a number of houses do not extend underground. Their walls rise at least 2 m above ground and the entrance is larger than it is usual in the *bayt al-qufl*.

The difference in house forms is basically related to the fact, already noticed above, that during summer only part of the local population migrates to the coast: as a consequence several dwellings are designed for permanent occupation, although they still preserve most of the typical features of the mountain architecture.

An outstanding example of the adaptation of the *bayt al-qufl* type of building to the function of permanent dwelling is offered by the houses of Harf Qabbi. The village is a *harah* of over 50 houses awkwardly built on the slope of a rocky plateau on the long promontory which ends with Ra's Sheikh Mas'ud, the northernmost cape of Ru'us al-Jibal.

The site looks utterly inhospitable, even by local standards. The only vegetation are two lonely trees growing on a patch of wind-blown sand. The bleak, barren ground has no other visible signs of life. Water is however available all the year round, preserved undeground where natural cavities have been hand hewn into enormous cisterns collecting the run-off of the entire plateau.

Sāl al-A'la, ruins of ancient buildings

118

Harf Qabbi, looking East

Harf Qabbi, looking North

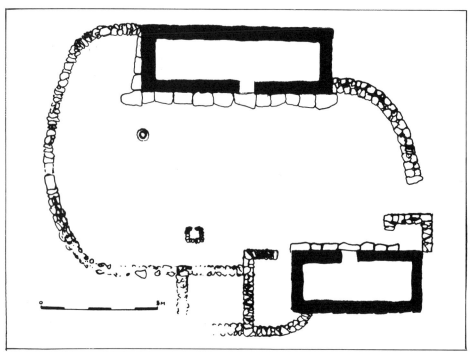

Harf Qabbi, house of Abdullah Mohammed Ali: plan

The village inhabitants are Ahl al-Harf, a subtribe or *batinah* of the Shihuh, to which belong also the communities settled at two sites on the coast: al-'Idah, a small cove on the western side of the promontory, and Hana, at the head of a bay some 4 km along the coast north of Khasab. Both sites have a small beach and wells with fresh water, but Hana has a wider hinterland with a palm grove and other cultivation.

The scenery at al Harf is grand and appealing with its breath-taking view over the two sides of the promontory and the rugged coastline of the Musandam peninsula stretching away to the horizon.

The village which once lay in total isolation is now touched by the new motorway and the distance from Khasab on one side and Bukha and Ras al-Khayma on the other has become negligible. Modern communications have given new impetus to local development and today almost half of the houses and a mosque have been recently built with imported materials and foreign style.

The 25 or 30 original buildings were a village of considerable size which existed in a sort of symbiosis with the coastal settlements of al-'Idah and Hana.

The architecture at al-Harf is quite interesting because it retains all the typical features of the Shihi house of the mountains but with the basic difference that is built entirely above ground.

As an example the house of Abdulla Mohammed Ali to the NE of the mosque was surveyed. The house complex covers an approximate area of 16 × 13 m and is centred on a rectangular courtyard defined and encompassed by two roofed buildings, standing on two opposite sides, and linked by a low boundary wall.

The roofed buildings have stone walls rising over 2m above ground and no openings except for the entrance which measures about 1.5 m × 0.8m. A single

Harf Qabbi, house of Abdullah Mohammed Ali, overall view from SE

panel door with wooden lintel is set only slightly recessed from the outer face of the wall and can be locked by means of a chained iron clamp secured by a padlock. In front of both houses run low stone benches, in proportion to the size of each building. The flat roofs are made of acacia branches supporting a layer of hardwood sticks, closely set and perpendicular to the beams, and a layer of mud mixture. Extra beams of smaller size are set in the roof projecting from the outer walls to form a ledge on all sides.

The inside of the house is divided into three sections: a central area with a fireplace, dirctly connected to the entrance, and two slightly raised compartments one at each end of the room: the one to the left of the door is used for sleeping and the opposite one, barred by a large palm stem grille, is used for storage.

Most of the architectural features of the house examined belong to the traditional repertoire of mountain architecture; only in one regard is the building alien to that tradition: there is no trace of the strong, almost obsessive concern for security, which is the basic requirement of the mountain builders. Their idiosyncratic attitude, determined by a particular lifestyle and a harsh habitat has produced that amazing building that is *bayt al-qufl*.

The example of Harf Qabbi proves that when the same people are not compelled to abandon their homes and leave unattended all their family belongings and provisions, their attitude relaxes and the form of the houses reflects this change. From the architectural point of view the result is a little disappointing because the buildings appear to have lost a relevant aspect of their original character without having replaced it with any new form elaborated in a different social and physical environment.

The average house of Harf Qabbi is a building of mediocre quality but is nevertheless interesting: in its undefined position between the fully characterized buildings of the mountains and the architecture of the coastal villages, it may help to understand some of the problems posed by the achitecture of Musandam such as the origin of the enigmatic houses of Kumzar and the humble and austere houses of Bukha.

Harf Qabbi, interior of house of Abdullah Mohammed Ali

Harf Qabbi: elevation of main building of the house of Abdullah Mohammed Ali

122

A presentation of the architecture of the Musandam mountains, even within the limits of these brief notes, would not be complete without mentioning the role played by the Shihi builders in shaping the rural landscape.

Beside the small cultivations which are always associated with the mountain settlements, a number of larger agricultural villages located at particular suitable sites, have fields of considerable surface area laboriously walled and terraced. Even these fields are irrigated exclusively by run-off, but for the exceptional size of the investment they involve elaborate and extensive systems of catchment, conservation, and distribution of water.

At the village of Fayd the terraced fields include some large silt flats created by dams of remarkable size. The village is perched on the top of the mountain range to the east of Khasab overlooking Khawr Habalayin, the large bay to the east of the Mablaq Isthmus: a spectacular setting which has no parallel in the area.

The village of Fayd

The delicately balanced ecosystem of Fayd has survived for centuries within the limits of what can be defined as a relative prosperity ; the seclusion is now over with the implementation of plans of assitance by the Government Aid Services. Fast communications, ensured by regular helicopter flights which provide periodical supplies, medical care and emergency transport, are a dramatic solution to the burden of age-old problems, achieved with the help of foreign technology, but perhaps less shocking and surprising than at first may seem: people are now so used to see aircraft about that they surely consider the landing helicopter another gift from the sky, just like the rain.

Run-off is collected and channeled to the fields and to storage tanks. In the direct use of water for irrigation, efficiency depends on four basic factors: correct position and design of the catchment structures, length and gradient of the distribution channels, appropriate position and design of the water inlets and finally perfect levelling of the plots' surface.

Due to the scarcity of rain any fault in the construction of the system and its adaptation to the topography may cause a considerable drop in the available amount of irrigation water and therefore a reduced agricultural yield. Imperfect levelling of the fields may on the other hand produce uneven distribution of water over the surface and unsatifactory growth of crops.

Fayd: most of the houses are built for permanent habitation

The fact that most of the population of Fayd lives permanently in the village and the fact that the site is practically inaccessible have strongly influenced the local architecture: most of the houses are built above ground, have large windows and occasionally loggias and covered terraces.

To the present writer's knowledge one of the largest field systems of the Musandam mountains is associated with the settlement of Sabtayn, located some 10 km inland of Khawr Mala on the Gulf of Oman.

Formerly totally isolated in the middle of the mountain range which divides the large Wadi Bih from the eastern coast of Musandam, Sabtayn is now reached by the new motor road built by the Government.

It is practically one vast farming site and its 15-20 houses scattered among the terraced fields are inhabited only in winter. After a good rainy season the yield in cereals (mainly wheat, barley and millet) is considerable and the buildings there act more as granaries than houses.

View of Sabtayn

Seasonal village of Sabtayn

Sabtayn, granary (yanz). Axe leans against sealed door (handle 85 cm long). Note figure of a horseman pecked on a large black stone next to jerz

The granaries, called *yanz* (a term common throughout Musandam) are cubic stone buildings measuring about 2 m on the side. A small square opening near the top, in the middle of one side allows for the operation of moving in and out the grain which is stored in sacks. The opening is carefully sealed to keep animals out not only when the granary is full, but also when it is empty so that it remains clean and ready for use.

At Sabtayn almost all the houses are of the *bayt al-qufl* type. There is also a multi-storey tower: at the base there is a semi-subterranean room of the *bayt al-qufl* type, on the second floor there is a room with access from outside and the third floor is probably a terrace with access from the room below. The building is made of blocks of decreasing size up to the walls of the third floor which are made of much smaller random stones. The tower is square in plan and rises with a marked tapering shape up to the third floor where the corners are rounded and the building becomes almost conical. From the dilapidated condition of the top of the building it is impossible to assess whether a full fourth storey was originally rising above the course of flat stones noticeable on the N side of the tower.

Sabtayn, multi-storey tower house

127

The tower of Sabtayn is a unique example of development of *bayt al-qufl* into a more elaborate building, probably owned by an important member of the community. For its size and character the building seems to reflect the importance and social background of the agricultural investment at Sabtayn, which almost certainly was constructed as a one-family venture. In many ways Sabtayn is the best example of the type of temporary rural settlement of the extraordinary beduin/settlers who live in the Musandam mountains.

Houses of Sal al- A'la, one of the few permanent settlements of the Musandam mountains

Taqada: a tiny seasonal settlement of the interior. On the right hand side the new motor road can be seen

The size of the field area of small seasonal settlements can sometimes be remarkable like in this small hamlet near Jabal Harim

130

At Sal al-A'la a silt plain of about 35 hectares supports very large trees. During the winter season the ground is covered with grass

Inhabited from time immemorial, the site of Sal al- A'la bears traces of ancient field systems and water channels

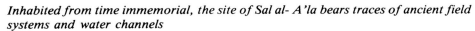

Water collecting system and reservoir of Khalidiyah, at Sal al- A'la

Water tank at al-Rawdha. Disused sinc long and partly silted up, the tank was the major source of water for a few families

Tiny seasonal field in the hinterland of Khasab. After the rains, the low stone walls are topped with thorn branches to protect the crops from goats. Runoff water flows into the depression visible in the foregroung and enters the field through square openings in the wall

Seasonal field near the mountain village of Rubi. The dry-stone wall rests on a carefully built footing which is fully visible on the inside of the structure

133

Mountain house with open courtyard. The house is partly obscured by the wall of the saffah, *or verandah, which was unroofed when the photograph was taken*

Most of the mountain settlements include small family graveyards. Although without inscribed tombstones, the graves are carefully built and the surrounding ground is paved with flagstones

A deserted roofless house shows how a bayt al-qufl is built: the inner floor is about 1 metre below surface and the sides of the house are lined with large stones. One foot above the floor level and on either of the short sides is a platform with storage jars. On the right is the small entrance into the building with a sturdy acacia door extending to floor level. The roof beams are twisted acacia trunks resting on an indentation at the top of the wall which is lined with slightly recessed stones meant to frame and contain the earthen roof

House with cyclopic walls near Wadi Bih and Wadi al-Rawdha junction. Built on the rocky slope of a low hill, the house could not be sunk in the ground and the builders obtained wall strength exclusively through the large size of the stones quarred nearby. Note the huge stones employed in the construction of the retaining wall of the terrace. A 10-year old boy gives the scale for the blocks framing the entrance

Permanent dwelling of Sal al-A'la. The house is almost totally built above ground and has a small window at the corner: an exceptional feature in a mountain settlement. Note the wall of roofless saffah which was opened on the two short sides and the protruding frame of the house roof

Abandoned bayt al-qufl in the al-Rawdha bowl. The building was left by an emigrated family probably shortly after having been built. The walls extend barely one metre above ground and the entrance is accurately sealed off. The surrounding ground bears no traces of courtyard and out-of-door areas and the building has the sinister aspect of a tomb

Sal al-A'la. In the background a large permanent house with full-sized entrance and terraced forecourt. The wing of the house extending to the left is a fully-built and roofed saffah *whose front wall has a square window and several small openings. The building visible on the left of the photograph is on the contrary a classic* bayt al-qufl, *with the usual low walls and tiny door (note hat for scale)*

Harf Qabbi: clustered on a rocky plateau overlooking the northern coast the village enjoys a superb view over the Strait of Hormuz and the coast of Iran which can be distinctly seen in a clear day

Large storage jar preserved in a ruined bayt al-qufl *of al-Rawdha (50 cm scale). Due to its large size the pot had to be put in the house before the building was completed*

Inhabited all the year round, the houses of Harf Qabbi, although basically similar to the mountain dwellings are built above ground and without the massive roof and the small recessed entrance which are typical features of the bayt al-qufl

In the past the inhabitants of Harf Qabbi could communicate with the coast only through a precipitous path to the village of Hana. The new motor road brings today imported commodities such as cement, gas cylinders and plywood, producing new life-styles and new building methods

A well at al-Alama: the small village, perched on a high mountain in the hinterland of Limah is inhabited during winter by potters who use the red clay obtainable in the area

Al-Alama. One of the many small water tanks used by the local potters who exploit natural fissures and cavities in the ground to store rain water (note the bag for scale)

141

Discarded pots left over at al-Alama. They include: cooking pots, coffee pots and incense burners. Baking is on open fire and waste is considerable

*A granary (*yanz*) at the seasonal village of Sabtayn, off Wadi Bih. These tower-like buildings, whose numbers betray a rich agricultural yield, are kept accurately sealed to keep animals out*

Al-Alama. Hand quern: the upper stone is rotated by means of an eccentrically positioned handle-bar which greatly improves the performance of the machine and reduces human energy

THE CRAFTS
by Gigi Crocker Jones

The following contribution on the crafts of Musandam is based on three five-day visits to the peninsula in February 1986, February 1987 and July 1987. These visits were made possible, and were accomplished under the auspices of the Musandam Development Committee. The author has spent some years studying the crafts throughout Oman. It is a pleasant and unexpected surprise to find that a few traditional crafts are still being made in the Musandam peninsula. However, the progress and resulting improvements in communications over the last ten years have inevitably led to an increasing market for consumer durables and items of man-made fibre, equally inevitably this has had an adverse effect on local craftsmanship.

There is still evidence to indicate that some craft items are in current use and that a number of people - usually the older members of society - are actively engaged in their manufacture.

PALM WORK

The cultivated date palm tree *Phoenix x. dactylifera* has traditionally and for many generations been put to a large number of uses. Of the remaining crafts in Musandam, palm frond work is the most evident. Some, though by no means all of the artifacts (especially household utensils) are discussed.

The cultivated date palm is grown in gardens adjacent to the houses in villages that are irrigated. Nomads as well as villagers own houses and date gardens in Khasab. So the date palm is used by everyone and all parts of it are put to good use.

The Artifacts. Basketry is known to be one of the earliest crafts and several methods of construction are evident in Musandam. The term 'palm work' will be used in this paper rather than 'basketry' as some artifacts are difficult to categorise as basketry. The braided artifacts which are made are functional items, and vary in degree of decoration. They consist of mats on which to dry fish and dates, food mats, food covers, carrying baskets of various sizes, weighing baskets, fans for cooling people and food, and date sacks.

A few years ago and certainly before 1970 useful items were made: shelters,

145

floor and prayer mats, a greater variety of baskets including cosmetic cases, those for keeping bread, for holding fish (these were tied to the boats); hats for wearing whilst fishing and possibly sieves.

Some decorative items which are still made in Bayah were traditionally made on the East coast only. These are the bridal bed canopy and wall panels for decorating a new home.

Functional items made from the rib of the palm frond may just still be found: fish cages for trapping fish and chicken coops for protecting chickens from predators at night or for retaining a chicken ready for the pot. Clothes fumigators are also made. Brushes made from the rib and the leaves are still in demand.

Bowls and containers, with lids, were made by the bedu using the coiling method. That is, a group of fibres are wound on top of each other starting from the centre: each row is stitched to the previous one as coiling continues. The core is of shredded *esqa*, the axis of the inflorescense (the thick portion of the stem from which the dates have been picked) of the cultivated date palm, which has been put in water and beaten with a stone. Stitching is of palm leaves from the same tree. The stitching fibre, sometimes coloured, covers the core completely. However, very few of these containers are available nowadays.

Men use fibre from the trunk of the palm tree for making ropes and cords and women use it for cleaning dishes and pots.

Braiding Processes. Fronds are cut from the tree with a curved knife with a saw edge. In Bayah, enough fronds for a year's supply are cut in the summer only and stored. In Khasab the fronds are cut at any time, all the year round. But the Kumzaris who live in Kumzar for nine months of the year and in Khasab for three months cut their fronds in the date picking season, i.e. between June and September.

Date gardens are usually inaccessible to vehicles, but as the gardens often adjoin the house the fronds can be carried home on the women's heads. Or the leaves are stripped off the rib, bundled up and carried home. Whole palm fronds are taken from Khasab back to Kumzar by boat.

The leaves are dried in the sun for one or two days in the summer and three to four days in the winter. After drying they are either dyed or stored. Dyes have not been obtained from plants within living memory in Musandam. The plants that were previously used in Dhofar were not seen growing anywhere in the peninsula. Chemical dyes, from India, have been available in the United Arab Emirates and can now be purchased in local markets in powder form.

Leaves are pliable whilst damp, but brittle when dry. To avoid damage they are dampened before braiding and stitching. They must also be dampened before dyeing to enable the fibre to absorb the dye. They may be dampened either by placing them in a bowl of water for a short time or by splashing water on them.

Leaves from different types of date palms are considered of equal value for palm frond braiding. But the health of the tree of course is important. Different leaves of the date palm are used for various specific artifacts. In order of preference these are: leaves from a seedling which are used for food covers, round fans for cooling food, small round baskets; newer leaves from the top of the tree, cut when slightly yellow are used for food covers, round fans, small round baskets and small food mats. These leaves are split into elements of just over 25 mm in width. Other leaves from the palm tree, cut when green, are used to make brushes, baskets and mats for various purposes. These leaves are split into elements of 50 mm in width. All the elements are approximately the same length of 50-60 cm. Using the centre rib of the palm frond involves, as we shell see, a different technique. It is used for chicken, bird and fish cages; the base of medium and large food covers; the backs of brushes; and for clothes fumigators.

The elements are braided into a long strip, measured at intervals, and finally stitched together. A narrow braid of 2 cm width is braided using the narrower elements: for the food covers, small food mats, round fans and round baskets. The elements are also used for the flag-shaped fan for cooling people, though the braiding technique is different. These elements are used double, i.e. one lying on top of the other. A slightly wider braid of 3 cm width is braided, using the wider elements for the carrying baskets and perhaps a medium sized food mat. A wider braid of 5 cm width, using the wider elements is braided for a large food mat. These elements are used three deep. The widest braid of 8 cm width, using the wider elements, is braided for a floor mat. These elements are also used three deep.

Traditional measurements are still used. They are: *shibr*, thumb to small finger with hand outstretched; *dhra'*, elbow to fingertip; and *ba'a*, fingertip to fingertip with arms outstretched. All measuring of braids is done in *ba'a*.

The designs are traditional geometric patterns, passed down from mother to daughter. In Khasab women stated that there are no new ones, and in Kumzar 'they don't get news', so they do not think of new artifacts or patterns. A commercial and enterprising braider in Bayah creates her own; for example, she had just braided the pattern of a curved dagger, *khanjar*.

In the past women spent much of the day making these artifacts for the home. With the increase in consumer goods the quantities produced now depend mainly on the commission given. The braider in Bayah stated that it all depends on people coming round and ordering. As far as she is concerned there is no limit. She makes 100 fans per month, and maybe 20 mats and food covers per month. Few commissions are given to braiders in Khasab. If there is a demand then 4-6 food mats per month are made. Water and electicity make household chores easier, so in Kumzar for example the women have more time; especially as the men are out fishing and the children at school. They thus can sew and braid every day. Women without children or with children who are grown up, have even more time. At present there is little demand, but the women are willing to produce more if they are commissioned to do so.

Production of most goods continues all the year round. However, a few items are seasonal and these are made in the summer only: fans for cooling people (though the braider in Bayah makes them all the year round and stores them until the summer), date sacks, back supports and ropes for climbing the date palm tree.

Production also depends on the migration of families. Traditionally the Shihuh are semi-nomadic, farming their small terraces in the winter and living by the sea in the summer so that they can fish and harvest the dates. If families have moved higher up into the mountains palm fronds may not be available. Or if they have moved to the United Arab Emirates other work may take precedence. The women of Kumzar produce items all the year round: in Khasab they braid from May to September and in Kumzar from September to May.

Women make the items from the palm frond leaves and the braids for the date sacks, but the men stitch them. Bedu women used to make the coiled containers. Brushes are made by both men and women, though are considered better when made by men who also make items using the rib of the palm frond, such as building material for houses and fishing huts, fences and gates; and for large date drying mats which are supported above the ground. Functional items made from the rib of the palm frond may just still be found: fish cages for trapping fish and chicken coops for containing chickens. There is possibly only one man remaining in Khasab who knows how to make a fish cage, and one other who knows how to make a chicken coop. Five years ago the fish cage maker made many cages. He could make one fish and four chicken cages in a day. Three years ago he made a few, but now makes hardly any as there is no demand. Prices are the same whatever the size of the cage as for a smaller one finer strips of rib are required and the work is more difficult. A clothes fumigator takes longer to make. Men also make ropes and cords from the fibre of the date palm trunk, and back supports for climbing the palm tree.

This work is done by all age groups, except children in school. Although at Bayah the son helps his mother after school. Generally though, crafts are no longer passed down from mother to daughter and father to son when the children are at school. The Bayah braider started braiding 'when she came into the world' and she enjoys making things. In Kumzar, 'all women whether they are young or old whose eyes are good make things'. With the coming of education, the pattern of teaching craft skills will change.

There is little specialization in the variety of braided artifacts either by age or tribe or village. 'Musandam is all the same' was the opinion of some of the women in Khasab.

However, of the coastal villages, Bayah proved the exception. The bridal bed, *hagala* and the wall decorations for new homes are made in Bayah and possibly other villages on the East coast. The *hagala* is made by each bride-to-be and the other village women come to her house to help. Palm leaves are braided into walls and a ceiling to enclose the bed leaving a door at one side. Colours are included. There is an opening celebration and others may look, touch or photograph but never enter. It is used by the bride and her husband for seven days and then thrown away - probably into the sea. The large wall decorations and the very long mat for the marriage are patterned with trees, khanjars and flags.

The quality of braiding may vary between villages, between tribes, and between settlers and bedu. This will depend on the skill and the interest of the braider as well as the quality of the leaves. The shape of the artifact will be similar, but the handwork and the quality of leaves will vary. The Kumzar women certainly use finer elements, braid more tightly and use more detailed patterning. The colours are standard as all markets sell the same dyestuff. The women do not mix them.

The artifacts are made by most women for use in their homes. Some artifacts are commissioned and some may be made 'to kill time'.

Food mats are placed on the ground and the tray of food placed on the top. People (men and women separately) sit in a circle around the mat sharing the food from the tray. Various sizes of mats are made in order to accommodate varying numbers of eaters. Food covers cover the trays or dishes of food in the home or outside when food is carried on the head.

Lesser varieties of baskets are used today. The Bayah braider is certainly making fish baskets, *jebban* for picked dates, and *makfa* for carrying anything in the home. The *meezan* for weighing may no longer be made, and the *habba* cosmetic basket is not - unless specially ordered. Round fans, date sacks and brushes are still used, but very few palm chicken coops are evident in the gardens.

Some artifacts are made specifically for the dowry; in Bayah the bridal bed, a wall decoration and a long mat; in Khasab, though perhaps not nowadays, food covers; *simma*, a mat for outside; small baskets with three ropes tied together with a rope handle on top; and in Kumzar bobbin lace braid for clothes and masks.

Gifts are given to parents and friends. And especially to visitors from elsewhere who do not know the palm frond braidings. Palm frond braidings are not exchanged between villages, except as gifts.

Artifacts are mainly sold in the United Arab Emirates markets by husbands or male family friends who are travelling to the U.A.E. The back support straps for climbing the palm trees made in Bayah are sold in Ra's al-Khaymah. Some items are locally commissioned such as the food mats and covers. Many people commission or buy directly from the house of the Bayah braider and the Khasab brushmaker. Few of these artifacts reach the local market.

Imported substitutes for braided items are cheaper, often stronger and more durable and they are easily available in the local markets, the U.A.E. and Muscat.

Plastic floor mats, thick carpets and linoleum have come to replace the braided floor mat; covered foam mattresses replace the sleeping mat and acrylic blankets replace the handwoven ones. Plastic bowls and buckets in bright colours are available to replace coiled pots and various braided containers. Air conditioners and electric fans render the braided fans obsolete. Nylon thread in various thicknesses is available for braiding: a date picking basket made from this lasts for five years instead of one. But for stitching this thread is certainly visually inferior to the palm-frond cord. Wire cages have replaced those made of palm rib, and plastic has replaced the rib of clothes fumigators.

Often the craftsmen and women are aware of the loss of quality and they are prepared to use the old materials if requested. As the brush-maker commented while binding his fronds together with cord of natural fibre 'other people may use nylon thread and other inferior materials nowadays'.

TEXTILES

Animal and plant by-products were used to provide the bedu and villagers with the raw materials for many of their basic needs: shelter, domestic utensils and trappings for camels and donkeys which were used for transportation.

There is little remaining evidence of textiles made from animal fibres in Musandam today; neither in the valleys where village families used animal trappings on both camel and donkey; nor it would seem, higher up in the mountains where donkeys (or humans where the terrain is too difficult for donkeys) were the beasts of burden. Camels are no longer seen and motor transport has in many cases supplanted the donkey. Higher up, commodities, such as cement, are now transported by helicopter.

Camels are known to have been used in Musandam in the past around Bukha, Khasab and Wadi Sal al-A'la, but they have not been seen for some years. No evidence was found of any artifacts made of camel wool.

There are few sheep in Musandam and there is no tradition of spinning wool on a spindle within the villages. There is of course amongst the bedu, of whom both men and women spin. Nowdays only the very poor still spin.

Long-haired goats are kept, though with increasing development it is becoming more difficult to keep goats within settled communities. With the advent of man-made fibres, goat hair has not been spun into ropes by the village men for fifteen to twenty years. However, the bedu continue to make them, as their livestock numbers are greater. Both the men and women amongst the bedu spin goat hair, though now it is mostly the women who do so. The goat hair is teased into a series of a form of rolag, *flij*, in preparation for spinning.

Goat hair is left undyed. White sheep wool was dyed with madder, *fua*, (*Rubia tinctorum*), and evidence of this was seen in an old sheep wool blanket found at Bukha. The madder colour resembled that obtained from the roots of the natural plant, not the chemical dye.

The cotton plant was not seen in Musandam. Cotton was bought in all the markets twenty to thirty years ago. It was spun by the men and made into fishing nets. There is no evidence of pit looms that could have been used for producing cotton cloth in the towns.

Weaving. Weaving is one of the world's most ancient crafts. But the villagers here have never woven either with sheep wool or goat hair. Looms were not seen amongst the bedu in the wadis and low lying areas. Ground looms are still in use high up in the mountains, but only to a very small extent, as substitute items can be bought in the markets. Access to these areas is difficult and therefore the author did not have the opportunity to see any weaving at al-Alama or Limah on the coast. Coastal villages are often only accessible by sea.

The ground loom is a simple device for keeping the warp threads under tension and consists of parts that are easily found, requiring little preparation or finishing. In Musandam these parts are made from *sidr*, (*Ziziphus spina-christi*) and *mizzi*, (*Amigdala arabica*), and include the following: four stakes, *witid*; two beams each called *dhabth al-wud*; a heddle bar, *missuk*; a shed stick, *missulla*; and a stick shuttle. Only the sword beater is carried; this is used for separating the warp threads each time the shed is changed, and for beating down the weft. In Musandam the two beams of the ground loom are usually short in length: 30-40 cm. Therefore only a very narrow width of cloth may be woven.

Weaving involves two sets of yarns, the warp and the weft, which interlace with each other. The loom-woven items in Musandam are made in a warp-faced plain weave, where because of the sett, the warp conceals the weft. Several items are made on the loom, though there are few signs of them today: a goat hair rug, *fili*; a blanket/shawl, *abeih* of sheep wool and a goat hair saddle cloth, *bardaa* for a donkey. These may still be found in inaccessible areas.

There is little evidence of loom woven or braided animal straps. Where the donkey is still used, the trappings are more often of sacking, commercial straps and nylon ropes. The *flij* and *abayah* have been replaced by imported rugs and blankets of man-made fibre.

Slings of goat hair or palm fronds were not used in Musandam for herding animals. But small sticks of *sidr* are used; not for hitting the animals, but to wave in the hand. Stones are used for controlling more distant animals. Vocal calls are used too for herding. These differ for camels, sheep and goats. There are two or three calls for each type of animal.

Braided straps for hanging the drums are still used. Though often now the yarn is acrylic rather than of sheep wool.

Cotton was imported from India in large bales of one *ba'a* width: (an Arab measurement - fingertips to fingertips with arms stretched sideways). It was spun on a spindle, but rolled along the thigh, to make a fine single yarn. This was wound off the spindle into a ball. Four singles were cabled together and then dipped in fresh water, doubled over with the two ends meeting and pulled taut; it was then massaged with a rag from one end to the other and left to dry. This yarn for making nets is called a *bug*. The needle is often made from the axis of the inflorescense, *esqa*, of the cultivated date palm.

In Khasab it is reported that bales of cotton have not been imported for about twenty five years. However, there is still some spinning of cotton for small gauge fishing nets in the coastal villages. Apparently this spinning is done by the women. Since 1970, imported nylon nets have been used. However, much time is spent repairing them by hand.

Cotton nets are often dipped in a solution to strengthen the fibre against the salt water. The ingredients of this solution will vary according to what is available in different areas of Oman. In Musandam, the plants and roots (or old trunk) of a date palm tree are gathered together and burnt. The resulting ash is called *huk*. It is beaten and the fine powder (unsieved) is placed in a cement container. Sea water is added and mixed. The net is put into this solution, left for a maximum of half an hour and removed. This process strengthens the cotton threads, but does not change the colour. It is repeated every two to three months or even every two to three weeks if the fisherman really wishes to preserve his net. This will depend on how many times the net is used per day.

The style of the women's clothes in Musandam is influenced by the United Arab Emirates. Neck openings of dresses run from one side of the neck rather than from the centre front as they do in Oman. Dresses, *disdasha mal harim* and comfortable pantaloons, *sirwal*, made at home use imported synthetic cloth mainly from China and Japan (previously from India and Pakistan); or they are made to order from an expatriate tailor or purchased from the Emirates.

Hand embroidery of clothes has virtually ceased since the advent of the sewing machine. Women's pantaloons may be machine embroidered sometimes with floral patterns, a work usually done by expatriate tailors; often the cuffs are machine stitched by the women using silver metallic threads.

Imported coloured cotton threads, and gold and silver metallic threads are used in the making of bobbin lace for their masks and dresses. Cloth of man-made fibre for dressmaking is imported and often purchased by husbands or brothers whilst working or visiting the U.A.E. or Muscat.

Surprisingly, the women do not embroider the caps worn by men, which are known locally as *kafiyah*.

POTTERY

Pots were, and to a much lesser degree, still are made at al-Alama and Limah. The clay was collected from a certain mountain top and surrounding plateaux in the form of dry soil. The men carried it on their shoulders, eight to twelve kilograms at a time, to the village of al-Alama. Clay was also collected at Qabal for the potters at Limah.

The clay was pounded in a dry state in a large wooden mortar made of *sidr*. It was then sieved through a piece of fine cloth and mixed with water. A pot was made immediately after the clay was mixed, as if left, the mixture was spoiled.

The pot was made on a wooden base; the base did not move. Each pot was moulded by hand commencing from a lump of clay for the base. The pot was built up by means of the coiling technique: a lump of clay is rolled in the hands to form a cylindrical shape. This is coiled round and round on top of itself. More coils are added as required. A piece of flat wood-was used to support the outside of the pot, whilst the palm of the other hand moulded the inside of the pot. Brims were made on the pots to facilitate their carrying.

The number of hours required for making a pot of course depended on its size. A small pot could be made in one and a half hours and therefore in a single session. A medium sized cooking pot would take two hours; therefore fifty per cent of the pot would be made in one hour on the first day and the remaining half would be made on the second day. This ensured that the first part was dry before commencing the second part, thereby avoiding collapse. The largest cooking pot needed for feasts is fat in shape and holds twelve kilograms of rice or sixteen of meat. Two and a half hours over three days are required to build this pot: one hour on the first day, another hour on the second day, and half an hour on the third day. The large barrel-shaped pots for storing dates, salted fish, rice, wheat and water are about 125 cm in height. They take six hours to build at the rate of one hour per day.

The pot is fired the following day when it is dry, as leaving it will cause it to crack. Pots are placed individually on burning logs of *sidr* in holes in the ground and removed when cool.

After firing the pot is of a yellowish colour, and it is then painted with a finish called *mshak*, possibly derived from the plant of the same name (*Fagonia indica*). The paint powder is red in colour and of a dry claylike material, to which water is added and mixed, and the resulting solution is applied to the surface of the pot as decoration. The pot is not fired again.

Large pots for storing dates, salted fish, rice, wheat and water are no longer made. All the bedu spoken to had never bought large pots from al-Alama in their lifetimes. Bread making bowls, small cooking pots, various incense burners and other small items are still made. Many pots have been imported from Iran. As with other crafted artifacts much of the domestic pottery has been replaced by modern substitutes: storage jars by refrigerators, plastic containers and buckets; clay coffee pots by thermos flasks and clay coffee cups by china; cooking pots by aluminium, and dishes and jugs by their plastic equivalents.

LEATHERWORK

When a goat is slaughtered it is hung up and the skin removed. It is important that the skin remains whole as a tear will necessitate patching. Salt is applied immediately.

At a later stage the hair is removed. The skin is placed in a pot of water early in the morning. It is left for the day and in the evening it is pressed and rubbed. Crushed, new green shoots of *alaq*, more commonly known in Oman as *ghalqah* (*Pergularia tomentosa*) are added to the water immediately. Any bits of *alaq* are removed and the skin is left to soak until the following morning. The hair is then easily rubbed off.

If skin containers are required to hold drinking water or milk another stage must be completed. This is a long process when *qaradh* (*Acacia nilotica*) pods are used. This process is necessary in order to keep the skin supple and so that the leather smell does not flavour the contents.

Once the skin has been removed from the *alaq* lotion, cleaned with fresh water, immersed in salty water and dried in the sun, full *qaradh* seeds which have first been crushed and pounded are applied. More water is added and the skin rubbed and left in the solution for two days; after which it is removed, rinsed and hung in the sun to dry. It is then ready for use.

These are used as whole skins: large ones for holding and carrying water (*qirba*) on the back supported by a headband; or smaller ones carried on the shoulder when travelling. These were widely used in the past for their properties of cooling water quickly. Some of the bedu still use them. Whole skins are also used for carrying dates (*habban*) and making laban (*shikwa*). Other uses include making bellows and drum membranes; or being cut up into fine strips and braided for making belts, etc. Some still remember this being done with flints, though in the present day of course knives are used.

152

INDIGO DYEING

Indigo (*Indigofera sp.*) was used widely in Oman but the industry has declined rapidly and especially in the past fifteen years. In some areas it was cultivated by farmers who extracted the natural dye and sold it in tablet form to the professional male dyers in the towns. They used the dye to give cloth the dark blue colour that was so highly favoured for dresses and masks.

Indigo also grew in its wild state over large areas of Oman including some parts of Musandam. The women carried out the work connected with the wild plant. In Musandam the women no longer do so, though the plant still grows there, as the dye is imported from India. Their method of making the indigo, *nil*, tablets was similar to that of the cultivators in Oman though on a lesser and simpler scale.

In Musandam the whole plant, locally also called *nil*, was pulled up (usually the stems being cut) and soaked in fresh water for two days. The water at the bottom of the container would look blue, but the remainder (perhaps 65%) remained clear. This surface water would be removed and the plant residue and the lower layer of water poured into a tarpaulin container or a sack of thick cloth. This was then hung up and left to drip for one to three days depending on the weather. The residual paste was then put on a flat container to dry, but before drying completely it was cut into small cubes.

Indigo was used medicinally to cure skin diseases: women, girls and boys applying it to the forehead, behind and in front of the ears but not on the cheeks, while men would apply it to the forehead only if very ill. It was also used to cure wounds, such as after circumcision, or on a newborn's navel for fifteen days.

For such purposes, a piece of indigo was dipped in water and crushed on a stone or wooden plate, the resulting paste being applied to the skin.

Moreover, it was used cosmetically by women who applied it at night to the forehead and face on special occasions such as delivery, and washed it off in the morning.

ACKNOWLEDGEMENTS I would like to give my sincere thanks to the following people for their help and support, guidance and translating: J. Dymond, M.D. Gallagher, A.D.G. Gordon, Hassan Ahmed Taha, Ibrahim bin Abdullah bin Morad al Baluchi, Ibrahim bin Mohammed bin Ibrahim al Shehhi, Jumah bin Said bin Masoud al Amri, Masoud bin Sulayman bin Mohammed al Shehhi, Mohammed bin Ali bin Sulayman al Shehhi, Taha bin Mohammed bin Hassan al Kumzari, R.K. Vincent, Jr., Zaid bin Sulayman al Shehhi, and to all the craftsmen and women who generously shared their skills and gave hospitality.

153

Food covers. Made of braided palm-frond fibers either in their natural colour or dyed, food covers are important house items, used in every-day life to protect food trays when they are carried on the head outside the house

Small food mat, made of stitched braided strips. Food mats are placed on the ground under food trays and dishes

154

Roll of braid. With its patterns carefully measured the braid will be stitched edge to edge into a food mat

Food covers may be finished in two different ways: either with a ridge to give a flexible rim, or reinforced with splints from the rib of a palm frond. The splints are first tacked on rather crudely with thread, then carefully wrapped with single wide fibers in alternating colours

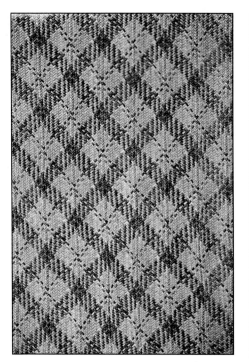
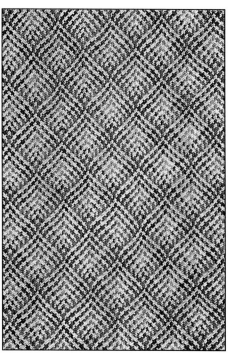

Various patterns of floor mats

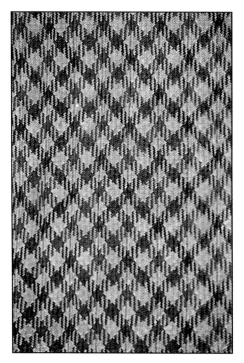

156

Fish traps on the beach of Bukha. Like chicken coops and cloth fumigators, tradi-tional fish traps are made with the ribs of date palm fronds. The ribs are soaked in water and then spliced into strips. Today fish traps and chicken coops are general-ly made with wire

Carrying basket. After the braid is stitched a two-ply cord made from date-palm trunk fibre is in-serted through the selvedges of the braids at right angles from the base of the basket up the sides to the handles

158

Wooden door with carved decorations found at Khasab. Ornamental motives and shallow carvings reflect the common type of the upper Gulf littoral.

Local timber and palm fronds still play an important role in the traditional roof construction. The stems of palm leaves neatly laid bottom next to top to compensate natural tapering, support a palm frond mat and a thick layer of earth

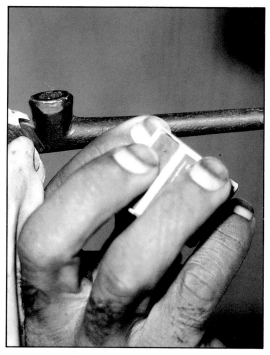

Small smoking pipes are among the traditional luxury items still made from wood

PALM WORK: BRAIDING

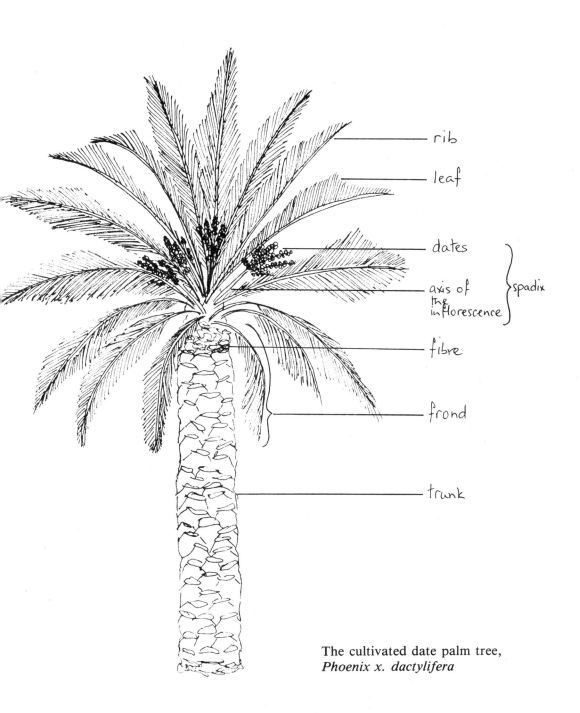

rib

leaf

dates

axis of the inflorescence

}spadix

fibre

frond

trunk

The cultivated date palm tree,
Phoenix x. dactylifera

In Kumzar chemical dye powder is added to the dyebath and stirred. The dampened palm frond fibres are simmered for a maximum of ten minutes, lifted out, and placed on sacking on the ground to dry. The dyed fronds are dried flat in the shade.

In Khasab not only the palm fronds are dyed but also part of a roll of braid. This has simmered for approximately ten minutes in the dyebath and is now lifted out using the rib of a palm frond. It is placed on sacking to dry in the shade.

The leaves are split whilst dry. Firstly the base is snapped off. Then the two sides of the leaf are pressed together, so that the leaf peels in half lengthways. The leaves are held in the right or left hand whilst the opposite thumb nail finely strips off the two outside edges. Now the thumb nail is inserted into the leaf near the base and several strands are shredded.

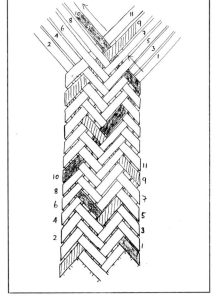

The element travels from the right edge over two, under three i.e. a twill weave, to the centre. This element becomes the last strand on the right of the left hand group. The braider pulls the left group and the right group away from each other in order to tighten the work. This is repeated from the left side.

As the work progresses the braider rolls up her braid, *dhafeerah*.

163

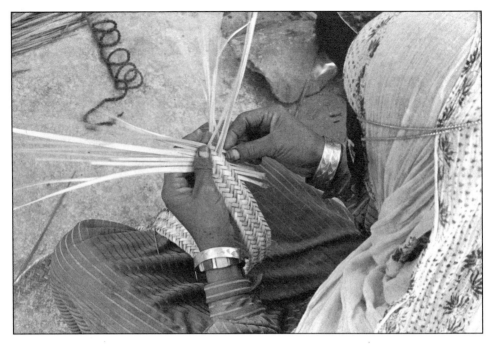

The braider holds the elements in her fingers and works away from herself. From a bundle of fibres by her side she adds a new element, *nasaa*, from the right hand side and places it on top of an already working element. This means that an element is added before the previous one is finished.

These samples of Kumzari braids illustrate the fine construction and delicate patterns used in this work. The two initial methods of braiding are shown. Braids with an L shape are stitched into artifacts that must start round and flat, such as food mats and baskets; straight braids are stitched into food covers.

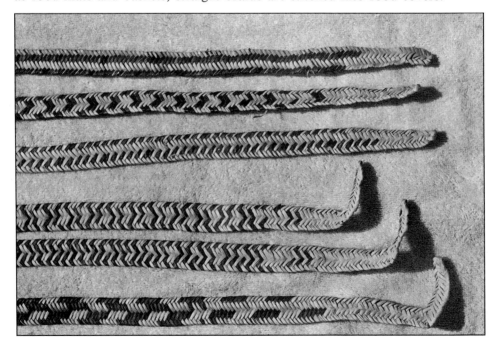

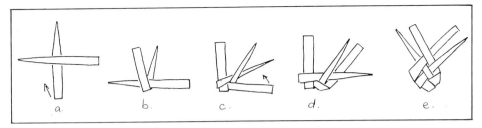

Figure above shows the commencement of a fine braid. The width and number of layers of each working element depends on the article which is being made. Work the sequence a-e and then spread out the elements which are three deep. Add new elements from the right, taking the new element under one, over one. From the left take the outside element over two, under two. Continue thus for approximately five cm.

The corner of the L shape is made as follows: with the work facing away from the braider and working from the left side only, the first left element is taken over one, under one until it reaches the extreme right side. This movement is repeated from the left twice again. Working from the right side of the braid the outer element goes over two, under two until it reaches the extreme left. Working from the left side the outer element again goes over two, under two to the centre. This sequence is repeated in the opposite direction and is continued until the required length of braid is made. New elements are added from the right side only, except when making patterns; colours may then be joined from either side. Each additional element is placed with the beginning overlapping the side. On the next row the element is adjusted by pulling it through to form a precise selvedge. The finishing end of an element is tucked under the braid out of the way. When the braid is finished, all the ends are trimmed by snapping off the dry fragments with the fingers. Scissors and razor blades are not used.

Braids are begun in a narrower width for one *ba'a* to facilitate a neater stitching at the beginning of the artifact. The depth of the elements are then spread out and extra elements added to widen the braid for the main part and drawn in again towards the end.

Two types of fans are made: the small round ones, *mishab*, for fanning charcoal when cooking and cooling the food; and the flag-shaped ones, *marwaha*, for human use. Because of air conditioners very few of the latter are now made. In households without electricity it is normal, in the summer, to have fans ready for one's guests. Note the technique is different in that the full width is braided. Very wide widths were also braided in this manner for placing on the supporting palm frond ribs to form the lower layer of ceilings, and these can still be seen in the old houses at Bukha. When the braiding of the fan is complete it will be attached to the rib of a small palm frond which forms the handle.

When the required length of braid is worked, it is stitched. The braid is wound and stitched in a circular movement from the centre.

Making the stitching cord.

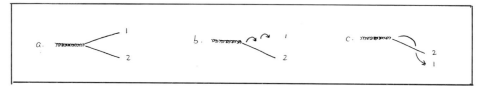

a.   Two fine elements of palm leaf will be twisted to make a cord for stitching.
b.   Turn element 1 clockwise twice.
c.   Bring 1 underneath 2 towards the body.

Repeat the same action with element 2, keeping the twists tightly together. Continue b and c until the required length is obtained, inserting a new element as needed.

Stitching used to be done with a fine cord of palm elements or single elements joined together with a reef knot. Green fronds were required for this, and a needle was not necessary. In Kumzar they used cotton thread, pulled from a length of purchased cloth, and stitched with a needle. Nylon thread is generally used now: it is considered easier and quicker.

Stitching the braid.

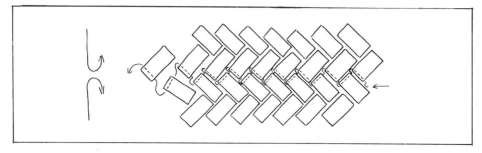

The braid is stitched edge to edge using every selvedge on both sides. This causes a slight ridge along the stitching line, but the thread should be invisible. Sometimes two selvedges of one braid are stitched to two selvedges of the other braid in order to manipulate a corner.

Whilst the braider joins the braids selvedge to selvedge, the upper braid is twisted upwards and the lower towards the braider. This facilitates the stitching process.

166

This neat roll of braid with its patterns carefully measured will be stitched into a food mat, *sarroot*. The L shaped end on the outside of the roll becomes the centre of the mat. The braid is stitched edge to edge using every selvedge on both sides.

Women make the braid for the date sack, *khasaf* using four elements in the left hand, five in the right and travelling over one, under one to the centre. The men do the stitching. They use a needle of *sidr*, (*Ziziphus spina-christi*), and stitch the braid which is wrapped around their legs eight widths high to produce the required sack shape. Dates are transported, sold and stored in these sacks.

The food cover may be finished in two different ways: either with a ridge to give a flexible rim, or reinforced with splints from the rib of a palm frond. The splints, overlapping each other, are placed on both sides of the rim and tacked on rather crudely with thread. They are then carefully wrapped with single full width leaves alternating the colours. The fibre may be stitched with a needle or pushed through, by hand, after the hole has been made with an awl. This method of finishing provides a firm circular base.

These three carrying baskets, *qafeer*, were made in Bayah. After the braid is stitched a two ply cord made from the trunk fibre, *leef*, of the palm tree is inserted through the selvedges of the braids at right angles. The cord travels from the base of the basket and up the sides to the handles. Often the rope for basket handles is wrapped in strips of cloth before plying to prevent chaffing the hands. Another typical basket (not shown here) for picking dates, *jebban*, is made with one handle from one side of the basket to the other. The picker climbs the tree, hangs up the basket and uses two hands to pick the dates.

This round basket was made in Khasab and used by women for keeping their cosmetics. In order to make the ridge around the basket perimeter the braider twists the left element in a circle towards her before braiding.

Round mats of varying sizes and uses are made with a ridge around the perimeter as described for the cosmetic basket. The ends are firmly plaited for a few centimetres and wrapped with an element of palm. The end of the element is woven vertically into the strips of braiding. Food mats are hung on the wall when not in use. Cord is stitched through the outer seams to form a loop. This loop may consist of anything that comes to hand, but ideally it should be of palm frond for the smaller mats and palm trunk fibre (to take the weight) for larger mats. Mats may have one loop, or two for carrying when doubled over.

Floor mats, with or without pattern, were previously made to cover the floor, often to the required length of the room and placed side by side to cover the width. They were thick and heavy. Lighter, and beautifully designed floor mats made in a village near Kumzar, are rolled out on a guest's arrival. They are braided in wider strips, which are stitched together horizontally with the outside braids ridged. Both ends are turned over once for approximately 6 cm and sewn with a running stitch.

The design on a Kumzari floor mat is delicate and detailed as shown here.

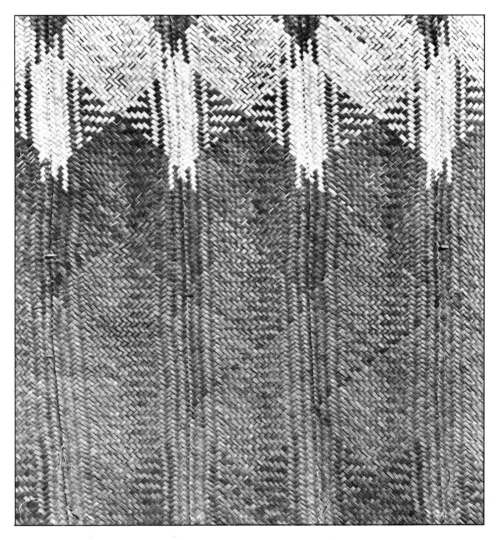

Sleeping mats, no longer made, have been replaced with foam mattresses. They were braided over two, under two, with eight elements in the left hand and seven in the right. Each element consisted of three leaves in depth. Twelve braids of approximately 9 cm width were joined together vertically to form a mat. Rolls of *simah* are still used for sleeping on in some bedu homes. Each working element is of three whole leaves in depth. These are braided using thirteen elements in the left hand, fourteen in the right, into a width of 10 cm and a length of thirty *ba'a*.

PALM WORK: BRUSH MAKING

The handbrush, *makhama*, which comprises one palm frond rib and two fronds with tied leaves is made as follows. Firstly each leaf is split into three. The fronds are placed in water for ten to fifteen minutes. Both fronds are then placed together and cut into quarters. Two of these are then placed together one on top of the other, and the leaves tied on the right of the rib. This tying is done with a single split leaf from each group: it is wrapped around the group twice and firmly tied with a half hitch. Each group of leaves is similarly tied. This section is exposed to the sun for two or three days.

Secondly, a rib from which the leaves have been stripped is cut into *dhraa* lengths (elbow to little finger tip). The rib is used as it is, or if too thick split in half. Four notches are cut equidistantly in each length.

Thirdly, the rib and the frond sections, from which the leaves have been stripped at one end to form a handle, are tied with cord along the four notches in a continuous length. On the first tie, sufficient cord is left to form a loop for hanging the brush. The cord tying is completed with two half hitches. The fronds are trimmed to an equal length. A craftsman can make fifty to sixty brushes per day. A brush takes four minutes to make and may last for fifteen to twenty days.

170

PALM WORK: CAGE MAKING

Chicken coops, fish cages and clothes fumigators are made with the ribs, *zura* (pl. *zur*) of date palm fronds. Two ribs are used for both chicken coops and fish cages. The leaves are removed and the rib sliced in half down the centre. The ribs are soaked in water for two days before being spliced into strips; some of which are kept long and some cut in half. Work for all types of cages is begun on the ground.

To begin the chicken coop, which in Arabic is called *qafas*, two parallel rib elements are positioned horizontally on the ground away from the coop maker. The nearest ends are held in position with the right toes. Elements are added alternately from the left and from the right. Figure below, left, shows this early stage, using interlacing elements on three axis which is common in basketry, with eight elements added.

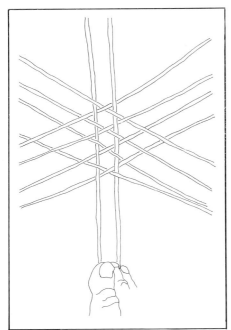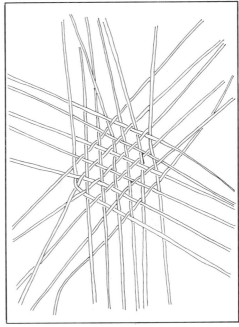

This is continued to a total of twelve, i.e six from each side. This base is now turned anti-clockwise through 90 degrees. An element is added from the left and woven in, and from the right and woven in. This sequence is repeated once more. The base is turned clockwise through 270 degrees. The left hand diagonal element is woven in a circular movement to the right in an open checker weave, as shown in figure above, right. Five extra elements, folded in half, are added roughly equidistantly from the edge of the base in order to increase the circumference of the coop. Weaving continues with the frame being turned round and round to the right in the maker's hands.

New elements are joined to old by overlapping. To finish, a border of three elements bound by a fourth is added to the weaving around the top. After trimming, the end of the final element is slotted back into the work. A lid, worked in the same manner as the base, is made to fit on the top and is secured with a 2-ply cord of palm frond leaves. A handle of the same cord is attached to the coop so that it may be hung up to avoid predators.

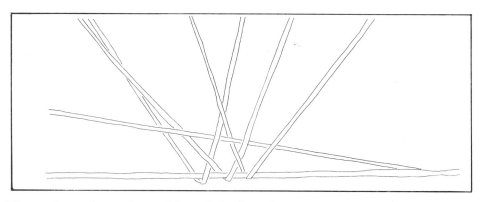

Figure above shows the position of the first elements for the beginning of a fish cage, *qarkur*. This is turned anti-clockwise through 90 degrees, and further elements are added to repeat the first sequence on the second side of the pentagon as shown in figure below, left.

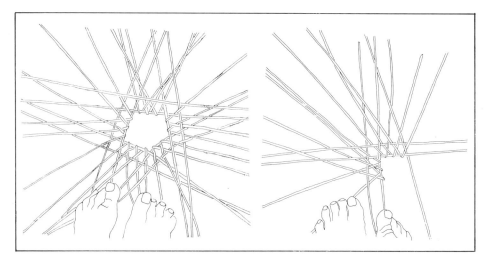

This action is repeated and the work turned anti-clockwise through each 90 degrees until the centre hole is complete as in figure above, right. These elements are now held in the hand and woven in whilst being turned round and round in a clockwise direction. New elements are added when necessary by doubling them over an element and twisting once. The shape is checked as the work progresses. At this stage it is put aside while the inner trap is made.

For this thinner strips of rib are used and a W shape with a flat baseline is formed leaving a space large enough for a fish to enter. The sides are woven together and work continues in a clockwise direction. The border is wrapped with a single element and tied with a half hitch knot. The inner cage is now tied within the outer with 2-ply cord.

The outer cage is continued and occasionally extra elements are added, doubled over and woven in to increase the circumference. When the cage reaches half its required final size (this is also the maximum circumference) a border using extra elements is made. The second half is made in a similar manner. A slightly curved triangular-shaped gate is also woven. This is to block the exit which is at the far end of the second cage. This gate is removed in order to take the catch out.

172

The two halves are bound together with 2-ply cord in a continuous widely spaced half hitch. Two parallel sticks of palm rib are lashed slightly protruding to the base of the cage. The triangular shape is placed inside the hole of the second half of the outer cage with the edges overlapping so that the fish cannot escape. It is held in place by weaving in two short sticks of palm rib set at right angles.

When in use this clothes fumigator, *mibkhara* is placed over the burning incense burner.

Four decorative panels are woven using five splices of date palm ribs. These are slotted into four supports of half ribs slit down the centre from the top to 20 cm from the base. The whole now shaped like a pyramid has a height of 55 cm. Strips of rib, covered in alternating rows of purple and green dyed leaves, are bound around the frame with 2-ply cord at the top and bottom of the panels and twice equidistantly in between. The base of the panels is also reinforced on the inside. At the second row from the top, a round panel of fine splices with a square hole in the centre is inserted inside the frame. The panel and the exterior purple

covered strips of rib are lashed to the frame at the same time. All the half hitch lashings are spaced at about 5 cm intervals. A loop of cord is tied at the top of the frame to facilitate carrying or hanging up when not in use.

PALM WORK: COILING

The core of coiled baskets are made from the axis of the inflorescence, *esqa*, of the cultivated date palm tree. This is the thick portion of the stem from which the dates have been picked. This part of the tree is only picked in the summer when the dates are harvested.

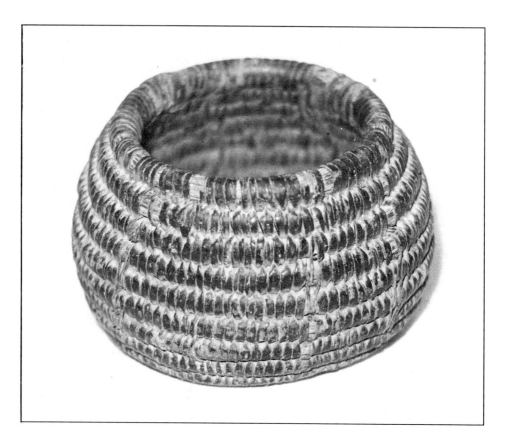

This round-based coiled basket, with a regular shape, is very neatly and firmly made. The foundation material is of *esqa*, finely split and bundled to form the core which is sewn in a spiral from the centre of the base. Split date palm leaves are used as the stitching material. The stitching element is wrapped around the core and stitched into the previous layer, as is each successive layer. A stitch, similar to lazy squaw but with the element partially split forming a V shape, is used. These are set at intervals of 5 - 7 cm around the circumference. These oblique lines thus created give a decorative effect as well as being part of the regular stitching. In this particular example the stitch has considerably worn away. The rim is finished by tapering the core, and is not reinforced with any extra stitching. This pot originally most probably had a lid.
Remnants of other coiled pots often have a thicker core, and some are decorated by the use of dyed stitching elements.

PALM WORK: ROPEMAKING

Local ropes, *habl*, are made from fibre from the date palm trunk as shown here. A piece of fibre, *lif*, is taken from the tree and wetted. It is teased keeping the fibres parallel. A piece is pulled out and twisted in the fingers. This is repeated until a group of rolags are prepared. Two rolags are placed together and held with the big toe. The spinner holds these two rolags, which lie parallel, in one hand and using his other hand on the top twists them separately away from himself; then giving a single twist in the same direction they are rolled together. All the rolags are used to form one rope. The ends of the rope are reversed so that the new end is held in the toes. Extra twists are put into the free end of rope. One third of the rope is folded over and twisted together to make a 2:2 cable and then the last third is wrapped diagonally round and round this to make a three cable rope.

In July and August the dates are harvested. Men climb the trees assisted by a back support, *sibta*, which enables them to have both hands free to pick the dates. This back support is made from rope using fibre, *lif*, from the date palm trunk with strips of cotton cloth and cord.

A piece of fibre is pulled from the trunk of the tree, wetted and torn up keeping the fibres parallel. A small bundle is rolled up the leg from ankle to knee while being turned in a clockwise direction. This forms a Z spun rolag. The rolag is reversed, if necessary, to twist it completely. A group of rolags are made, each approximately fifty cm in length.

The ends of two rolags are held with the big toe and twisted together in the palm of the hands, right hand over the left. The ropemaker twists the rolags in an S spin away from himself. Rolags are joined by overlapping a new one with the old, the new one being placed between the two in use. The rope is measured by *dhraa*; it needs to reach to the end of the date garden.

The cotton cloth is torn into strips and a stick inserted in the loop of a finished end of the rope. An assistant holds and turns the stick while the ropemaker wraps the cloth strips around the rope. The cloth wrapped rope is folded in half, and the two halves are wrapped around each other while the assistant unravels the two ends. These are then wrapped with cloth, inserted through the gap at the fold, and bound all together with the remaining cloth. To do this the ropemaker has to hold down the two loops with his foot: he must continue to do this whilst he stretches the loops.

The loops are then pressed together to form a long, oval shape. Using a wooden needle, *mabray*, made from *simr*, (*Acacia tortilis*) with thread of nylon or palm fibre cord the loops are stitched together between the twists to form a firm solid band. At each end loops are left open to form large eyelets, through which pass the thick date climbing rope. These two eyelets are bound with a blanket stitch worked closely together.

176

TEXTILES: SPINNING

A spindle, *maghzal*, with the whorl, *raghwa*, at the top of the shaft. The single, circular shaped whorl is unusual for Oman - the bedu use a single bar. However, it is typical of the shape of spindle used in Musandam. A hook is driven into the shaft, projecting above, and is used to suspend the yarn. Both the whorl and shaft are made from the *sidr*, (*Ziziphus spina-christi*). Most of the circular whorls are unpatterned. The goat hair single yarn, spun by a daughter of the bedu house-holder, is one to one and a half millimetres in diameter and will be made into a rope.

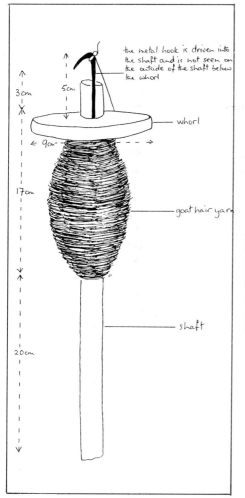

the metal hook is driven into the shaft and is not seen on the outside of the shaft below the whorl

whorl

goat hair yarn

shaft

3cm
5cm
9cm
17cm
20cm

This is another type of spindle, but it has a double bar whorl. It is used in the same way as the previous spindle, but it is unusual to find this type in Musandam and Oman generally. The *bedu* living around the edge of the Rub al-Khali are known to use them. It has proba-bly been purchased in Saudi Arabia.

To spin, the shaft is rotated between the thumb and forefinger, and then dropped to rotate freely. It is twisted in a clockwise direction to give a Z spun, single yarn. The same spindle is usually used for plying, sometimes using the same method but rotating the spindle in the opposite direction, i.e. anti-clockwise giving an S spun yarn. Yarn is most often plyed by rolling the shaft down the right thigh to give a firmer twist.

177

Figure above shows a warp-faced donkey saddle cloth, *bardaa* woven on a ground loom on two warps and divided into four pieces which are sewn together. The two outside panels are stitched together with an oversewn seam. The stitching of the centre seam and the edging is decorative as well as functional and is shown in figure below. Apart from seaming it is used to strengthen the edges of the saddle cloth and to protect it against wear and tear. The stitch is the same as that used on a camel saddle bag, *khurrij*, and a woman's bag, *khurrij mal harim*, in Oman. Handles, of buttonhole stitch, worked closely together, are added at the centre and along the sides. The cloth is without pockets. The yarn used for warp and weft is of a 2-ply goat hair. The saddle cloth is lined with two layers of blanket crudely stitched to the surface cloth with strips of material.

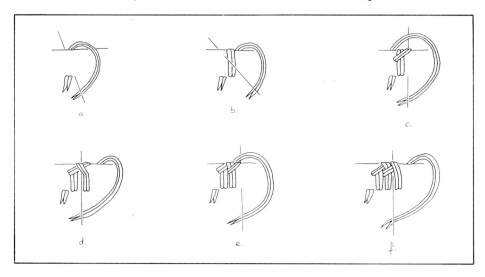

The donkey saddle, *shidad*, is made of wood from the *sidr*. The *shidad* and *sanaq* sections are tied together with rope of nylon or goat hair. The *tafar* is of two strands of cabled nylon, each cable is 3/4 cm in diameter. The cabled nylon is wrapped in strips of cloth providing a firm yet soft strap. It is two and a half cm in diameter and 100 cm in length. All the straps: girth, neck, headstall and rein, and hobble were previously of goat hair, but nowadays they may be of nylon or commercial canvas braids.

This saddle, *shidad*, is for a loading camel and is shown here supported by a cushion. It is larger than a donkey saddle. The *shidad* is 93 cm in length, the *sanaq* 29 cm high and 34 cm wide at the base. The *sanaq* is also decorated. Camels are no longer to be seen in Musandam and have not been used as beasts of burden for some years.

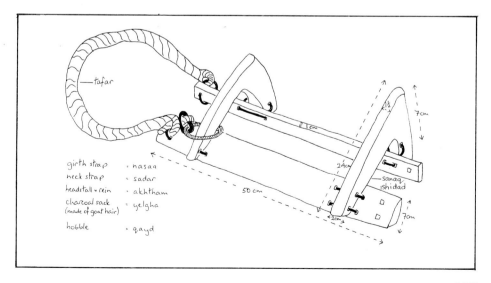

girth strap	= nasaa
neck strap	= sadar
headstall + rein	= akhtham
charcoal sack (made of goat hair)	= yelgha
hobble	= qayd

TEXTILES: NETTING

This must now be an unusual sight: here a Kumzari fisherman is making a net of cotton for catching sardines. In Khasab a fisherman explained that he has not made a cotton net for twenty five years. Almost all nets now are made of nylon: small gauge for catching sardines and larger for bigger fish.

A netting knot is made as shown in figure below. The mesh stick, *terak*, is held in the left hand and the yarn wound around it once. This is held firmly by the left thumb whilst two quick movements to the left and to the right are made with the right thumb. The netting needle is drawn through from behind the foundation loop. The knot is pulled, adjusted and pulled tight.

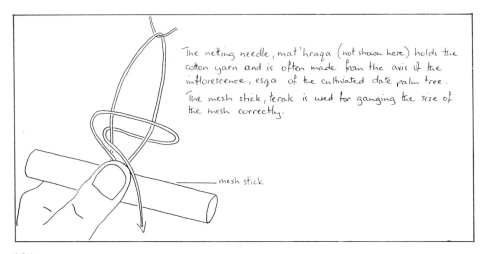

The netting needle, mat'hraqa (not shown here) holds the cotton yarn and is often made from the axis of the inflorescence, esqa of the cultivated date palm tree.
The mesh stick, terak is used for gauging the size of the mesh correctly.

mesh stick

180

TEXTILES: NEEDLEWORK

Non-restrictive clothing covers the body from neck to ankle and wrist as in the Muslim tradition. The head too is covered and often a mask is worn. The dresses are decorated with a six strand braid stitched by machine around the neck, front panel and the wrists.

The braids are made using the bobbin or pillow lace technique. A group of separate threads are fixed at one end. They are mounted and wound on to a padded cushion supported on a pedastal or tin. The other end is weighted by bobbins.

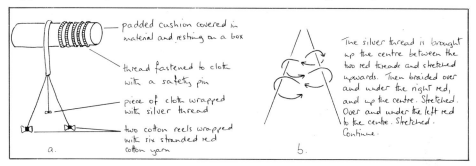

a.
— padded cushion covered in material and resting on a box
— thread fastened to cloth with a safety pin
— piece of cloth wrapped with silver thread
— two cotton reels wrapped with six stranded red cotton yarn

b.
The silver thread is brought up the centre between the two red threads and stretched upwards. Then braided over and under the right red, and up the centre. Stretched. Over and under the left red to the centre. Stretched. Continue.

To embellish the pantaloons, metallic thread is stitched by machine (without braiding) directly on to a piece of cloth. This is sewn on to the base of the legs of pantaloons to form a most attractive band of silver around the ankles. To ensure a snug fit the cuffs are fastened with studs or zip-fasteners. Modern cuffs are embroidered with a much deeper band of silver than they were in the past.

As in most areas of Oman, the women in Musandam now make their masks (with a stiffened centre protrusion) from imported cloth dyed with chemical indigo. A narrow braid, shown in figure above is made using two bobbins of cotton and

one of silver metallic thread. This is stitched in two loops onto the face masks. The braid is tied at the back of the head: the longer loop being inserted through the shorter and tied with the longer hanging down the back. A woman may make braids for her own use or to sell.

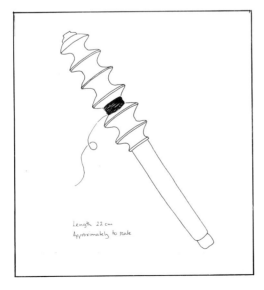

Length 22 cm
Approximately to scale

This bobbin *karar* was used for holding the threads when embroidering men and women *disdashas* and the cuffs of *sirwal*. It was extensively used before the advent of the sewing machine, but nowadays, if used at all, it is to embroider the cuffs of *sirwal*. This embroidery is called *durza*.

182

POTTERY

Coffee pots have largely been replaced by the thermos flask. But this is one example of a recently made pot in the traditional design. Note the decoration with *mshak*.

Cooking pots were made in different sizes, even very large ones for preparing wedding feasts. Only the smaller ones, such as this, are made nowadays. But the design and decoration remain the same.

An old pot for storing ghee from a house in Sal al-A'la.

These storage jars are exposed to the daylight as the room is being rebuilt. They are used for storing wheat or rice, except the jar at the centre back which is for water. They were made at al-Alama and are said to be over one hundred years old.

An example of the modern pottery are the incense burners available in consider-
able variety from al-Alama.

LEATHER

This most splendid piece of work from the village of Harf Qabbi was claimed to be a leather back-support for climbing the date palm tree. But it was surprising that such fine workmanship would be capable of withstanding such rigorous work. Further discussions revealed that it is a many-stranded leather back supporting cincture, *haqub*, worn around the loins under the *dishdasha* and over the loin cloth, *wizaar*. The skin is cut into strips and braided into sixty fine three-strand braids, each of 2 mm width. Each end of the cincture is finely worked with a single element of leather forming a strong loop.

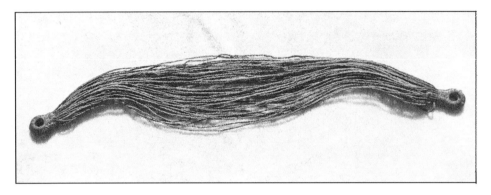

LEATHER: TEXTILES

This drum, *thabl,* made in al-Alama, is of *sidr* wood, and carved with a typical pattern. Goat skin membranes are stretched over each end and clamped with rings of *sidr*. The goat hair ropes are under tension and in turn keep the membranes taught. Ties, also made of goat skin, are adjustable for tensioning the ropes.

186

The warp-faced drum strap, *bilrah*, is woven on a ground loom using a pick up technique to make the pattern, known as *raqam*. Structurally it is known as a one-weft double cloth in which the back cloth is left unwoven. This leaves floats

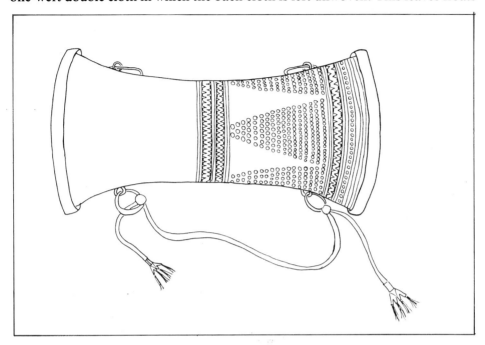

at the back, which have been covered by the strap lining. The strap was bought in Buraimi (from where many of the Omani textiles are sent up the Gulf) and was probably made by the Duru, a local ethnical group. The ends of the strap were finished in al-Alama; cotton yarn added and decoratively wrapped.

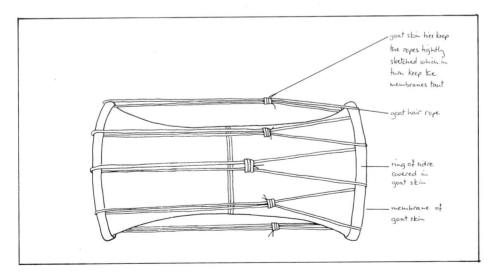

goat skin ties keep the ropes tightly stretched which in turn keep the membranes taut

goat hair rope

ring of sidre covered in goat skin

membrane of goat skin

It appears that the more traditional drum straps made in Musandam are braided in an oblique interlacing. An old flat braid of sheep wool using four colours, i.e. natural brown and white, dyed pink and green which have faded, has been worked with free elements, half of which run on a Z and half on an S slanting course. The outer element on the right passes over two, under two to the centre and becomes the inner element of the left group; then the outer element on the left is repeated in mirror image. This has created a zigzag pattern. Each element is of 2-ply yarn about 2 mm in diameter. The strap is 3 cm wide and 230 cm long, and is finished in two eight strand round braids with tassels at each end, though at one end the two braids are joined together, to make a loop before ending in a tassel. Additional yarn is added to each tassel to give extra bulk. Figure below shows the method of making an eight strand round braid and the final result.

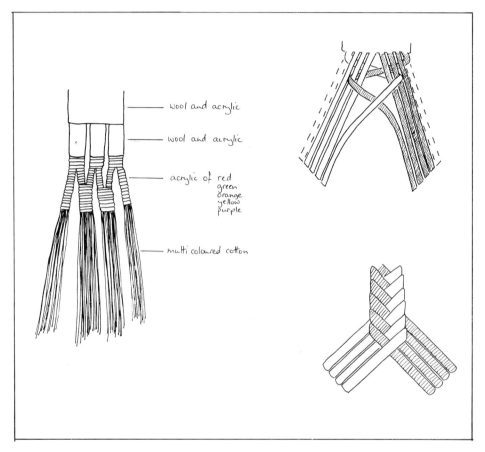

A drum strap with sixty one elements of acrylic yarns was being made by a woman near Jebel Harim. Paired elements passed over four, under four to the centre in a similar manner to the previous strap. However, the various colours are not well organised and create a disordered pattern. One end of the strap had been finished, firstly with two round braids combining to form one and then dividing to three containing 21, 18 and 17 elements respectively. This strap is 3.5 cm wide and in comparison to the former is of a spongy texture.

The drum, an important artifact in this culture, is still used especially at weddings. In 1987 it demanded the high price of Omani Rials 900.

188

Cowrie shells with the base cut off, are stitched on to strips of leather to adorn the bow and the stern of the boats at Kumzar. This is a symbol of past wealth and all around the Indian Ocean people traded for cowries. Both *Cypraea annulus* and *Cypraea moneta* are now rare and in fact are locally endangered species.

THE JERZ
THE UNIQUE SMALL AXE OF MUSANDAM
by Robert K. Vincent Jr.

The most unique and distinctive implement of the Musandam region is what is commonly called a 'Shihuh axe' locally called *jerz*. It is a small decorated hatchet fixed to the end of a stick cut from indigeneous wood.

It is used today mostly among the Shihuh in whatever area they occupy. The Shihuh are semi-nomadic people in that they abondon mountain and small fishing villages during summer to migrate to coastal areas for date-palm cultivation: consequently their areal range is quite wide. In addition to Musandam peninsula, they inhabit the northern and eastern areas of the Emirate of Ra's al-Khaymah, the Omani enclave of Mudha, which is an Omani 'island' in a sea of U.A.E. territory and further south in Oman the lands around Shinas.

The history of the *jerz* is obscure and is not elucidated by questioning local people and long term residents. Nonetheless, conjectures may be made.

Archaeological evidence exists in the form of axeheads that have been excavated from graves. The first dated to the end of the 2nd millenium B.C. was found at al-Khadra, (wadi Samad), a considerable distance (800 km) from Musandam. However, recent finds by archeologist Walid Yassin al-Tikriti of the Department of Antiquities of Al-'Ayn include the second and best example yet of the typological ancestor of the *jerz*. Dr. Tikriti's excavations of spectacular grave goods in 1987 were carried out at the village of Qidfa, on the east cost of the U.A.E., at the mouth of Wadhi Mudha, only 50 km south of Musandam proper. Some 16 axe heads were found. The beautiful bronze one illustrated here can certainly be considered precursor of the *jerz* because of its shape and size even though it doesn't have the hammer head of today's axes.

The date suggested for this axe is the second half of the 2nd millenium B.C..

Certainly one can expect that more axes from more recent periods will emerge from further excavations and thus provide a continuum style up to current *jerz*. The discovery of the Qidfa axe is confirmatory evidence that Musandam metal workers had a protoype on which to base the production of subsequent axes.

But the discovery of small axes outside Musandam proper, provides no real clue as to why the *jerz* appears only in Musandam and not, as one might think, in other areas of Oman. In order to seek an answer to the geographical distribution of the *jerz*, one should direct researches towards Persia, the closest point of contact along a trade route accross the sea. Until very recently (1983), Musandam was not accesible by road beacause of the formidable barrier of high cliffs abutting the sea. Import of goods to Musandam from Persia could have been confined by these same mountains, but these same goods could have been transferred further south along the cost of Dubai. Yet the *jerz* does not appear so far south, so other factors must therefore account for their presence within Musandam, only. A possibility lies in the reputation that the Shihuh have, as fiery warring and independent. Visitors to Musandam require no imagination to realize that the topography is very inhospitable and that special toughness and durability are necessary to survive there. Historically the Shihuh have had to defend themselves against interlopers and pirates. They must have inhabited the high, isolated farmsteads in the mountains partly for defensive purposes. These farmsteads are at such high, elevations and so far from the coast that raiders would have found it difficult to penetrate them. In their defence, the Shihuh would have used hand weapons, and some older residents recalled that the earlier days every male carried a sword and small shield in addition to his usual trappings of a knife and the *jerz*. So men were armed and ready for combat. As warring diminished, swords and shields became obsolete, but the knife and *jerz*, both less cumbersome and more portable and useful remained, a vestige of old weaponry and times.

In fact the *jerz* is very functional implemet. It is used as a walking stick in the very rugged terrain of these mountains and it offers solace as defence from the caracal lynx (*Caracal caracal*) and leopard (*Panthera pardus nimr*) which are known to exist to this day. It is used as a prop pole to hold sacks which are hung over the stick, and then slug over the shoulder. The *jerz* is also used as an ornamental accessory and brought to important tribal community functions. As has been said the *jerz* can be considered equivalent of the *khanjar* or dagger-like knife carried by the rest of the Omani population. Its use as weapon is not just vestigial though, and some cases of figting and scars resulting from wounds have been observed. In recent incidents of tribal fighting the *jerz* which comes readily to hand was an essential element of the fray, and the cause of hospitalization of some of the combatants.

The typical *jerz* is placed on top of a wooden shaft measuring about 83 cm long and 2 cm in diameter. A brass cap, about 3 cm high is placed sometimes at the bottom of the shaft to protect it from wear. Sometimes a collar is placed at the neck of the shaft where the *jerz* is fixed to a reduced diameter stem and secured by small nails. The wood shaft is cut from several indigeneous trees including the flowering bitter almond *Amigdala arabica*, known locally as *mizi* or *mizj*, and *Ziziphus spina-christi*, known locally as *sidr* from the coast. Usually small bands and Xs are incised into the shaft for ornamentation.

A typical *jerz* measures about 10 cm from blade edge to hammer head, and is 3.5 cm broad at the end of the blade and 1.8 cm at the hammer head.

The shape of the *jerz* is relatively the same on all examples. The features that most distinguish one *jerz* from another are designs of incision and inlay. There is no relation between a design and a tribe, or a geographical area. The different designs are found everywhere and comparisions with designs or other Omani metalworks have yielded little similarity. Other Omani weapons, such as swords, knives and khanjars have silver hilts and scabbards and steel blades. But the blades are not worked and the silver designs bear no relation to those on the jerz. Likewise there are no parallel designs on the wide variety of Omani silver jewellery except one class of bracelets from Sur and then only a minor pattern on its shoulder and not on its face. On brass work one finds a similarity only with the diamond pattern reminiscent of the work between blade and hammer on the *jerz*.

192

A modern jerz *held by Taha bin Mohammed bin Hasan al-Zarafi, a Musandam citizen from Kumzar*

This lack of parallels is striking and demonstrates the uniqueness of the *jerz* and the isolation of its production. Craftsmen working in metal could be expected to render similar designs particularly when similar patterns are employed. The difference may be attributable to the different malleability of the metals. Silver is softer than iron and lends itself to intricate designs. Steel needs to be forged, is hard and less flexible and only with even harder materials can cuts and grooves of simple, geometric design be incorporated. Also, patterns on silver are very traditional and conservative with little variation from basic type. A bracelet maker would not adopt the style utilized by a *khanjar* maker; so too the *jerz* maker may not have adopted silver patterns. Lastly the geographical isolation of Musandam from Oman proper may have prevented interchange of design. One could perhaps look towards Iran and Baluchistan for comparisons.

So it appears that the only factor to account for divergence of type is an economic one. If a man can afford it, he can buy an elaborate design, otherwise he has to settle for a cheaper, simpler one. There are 3 different types of design which are illustrated in the plates. They can be defined as: simple, incised and inlaid.

Simple

Pages 197 and 198 top illustrate this style. The blade has no decoration, rough-cut groves are notched at the front of, on, or behind the collar of metal that allows the *jerz* to be attached to the shaft. The hammer head is slight, acting merely as a counter-point to the blade and is barely functional. All of the *jerz* seen in this category were well-used and aged by pitting, corrosion and nicks and they may represent the earliest examples. They are most similar to the ancient Qidfa axe. The *jerz* seen on p. 198 top-right is transitional as it has sligtly more detail that the crude grooves.

Incised

The examples on p. 198 center and bottom and on p. 199 top, center and bottom-left have from crude to fine incisions on the blade or the collar or the hammer head, which is more developed and a feature in its own right. These incisions are all geometric and consist of straight lines, "V's", hatching, points and part circles. Figure on p. 199 top-right, which is a fairly crude axe, nonetheless has an inlay element, a feature of the most sophisticated *jerz*. Figures on p. 199 center and bottom-left represent the best of the incised category and have some inlay work.

Inlaid

It is in this style that there is the best work of the craftsmen (see p. 199 bottom-right, p. 200, and p. 201 top). Incisions are crisp and patterns are relatively complex, composed of shapes within shapes. Most of the blade and all of the hammer-based is worked. The hammer-head is developed into a significant feature of its own with indentations on either side marking its seperation from the collar. The head of the hammer and the top of the *jerz* are incised, too. the inlay work has 4 stripes; 2 on each side of the stick. each *jerz* has thickness, weight and heft, unlike the *jerz* in the other categories which are relatively slim and light-weight. Clearly, these heads with their full and well-executed ornamentation are made to be displayed. It stands to reason that these more expensive ornamental axes signify a period of both prosperity and peace. For at such a time, money could be spent on more expensive designs which would not be damaged by the rigors of defense or function.

194

In this category, one special *jerz* stands out because of the extent and the personalized nature of the inlay work (p. 201 centre). The name presumably of the owner who commissioned the piece, is clearly inlaid as Sayyid Mohammed Qataf.

At this point, a word or two about manufacture and materials is relevant. Most of this information was obtained during discussions with Rashid Seyf Al-Shamsi, of Bayah, one of the last two makers of the *jerz* who died in December 1986 (p. 201 bottom). He had manufactured *jerz* as part of the blacksmith trade which he started as a young man. His material has come always from scrap steel. First, it was left over from houses built for the Sheiks, then cars and machines and the new material that is very shiny and which is now very sought after by those who commission *jerz* today.

He made *jerz* as and when they were requested; thus like most village craftsmen, he reacted to the demand and did not manufacture to have a stock inventory. He indicated that he had made them to whatever design anyone wanted.

As he sold to any buyer according to whatever design they requested (and he remembered over 20 different ones), it is clear why there is no tribal or other cathegorized difference among the design for all designs were availble to all buyers; they merely had to pay the price. The material used for inlay work was brass from spent cartridges. He spoke rather disparagingly of the process of the only other *jerz*-maker, Abdulla Suleiman Bani Haraiz of Limah who did not forge his own but obtained them from a blacksmith and then imposed his own designs.

The demand still persists for *jerz* today and the one most sought after is similar to the very best traditional design. Most people however cannot afford the high price of Omani Riyals 100 for a hand-made *jerz* from Limah (p. 202 top). Instead four other types are sold in Khasab to be used by the Musandam inhabitants themselves as well as sold to tourists (Omani and expatriates) who are not from Musandam. The first type is a simple stamped brass *jerz* manufactured in India (p. 202 centre). It is fastened to a rather ornately machine-carved stick and sold for Omani Riyals 3.

Another model is forged in Limah and sells for only Omani Riyals 5. A third type comes from the U.A.E. and a last from Pakistan. The brass one is carried and used today in Musandam, but the others are not popular (p. 202 bottom).

The *jerz* then is evolving and, while its origins are obscure and the art of making them will die when the last maker dies, it has been regenerated as a symbol of the region. The local government authority incorporated one in its logo and erected 2 monuments at 2 roundabouts using it as a motif. One of the army regiments uses it likewise and crossed *jerz* appear on walls of various offices and residences (p. 203).

Of great interest still it would be to locate other antecedents of the *jerz*, particularly types provided with a hammer head. At this time it is still not known if the Qidfa axe is to be considered the oldest example or part of a continuum leading to the modern *jerz*. But surveys and excavations in Musandam may unearth the evidence and fill the gap in the chain of today's tradition from grave good to functional weapon and finally to ornamental walking stick.

Acknowledgements The author would like to thank the following for their assistance:
P. Costa, D. Critchfield, J. Dymond, M. Gallegher, Juma bin Said al-Amri, S. Kay, Khadem bin Suleyman bin Khadem al-Shehhi, Mehdi bin Mohammed bin Yusuf, The Musandam Development Committee, R. Redford, J. Sasser, P. Sichel, Taha bin Mohammed bin Hasan al-Zarafi, Walid bin Yassin al-Tikriti.

Khadem bin Sulaiman bin Khaden al-Shehhi, a Musandam citizen from Rubi village holding a jerz

Bronze axe head from a grave excavated at Qidfah, on the eastern coast (R.K. Vincent jr.)

An axe excavated from a tomb at al Khadra near Samad (Sultanate of Oman) dates to end of 2nd millennium b.C. (P. Costa)

A bronze axe excavated in 1987 in Qidfah, United Arab Emirates, by Walid Yassin al-Tikriti. Dated to the second half of the 2nd millennium b.C., this axe is clearly the precursor of the jerz *(courtesy of W.Y. al-Tikriti)*

196

Here the jerz *is used by Sultan bin Heimed bin Salim al-Shehhi to support a shoulder load. The axe is carried flat in the palm*

A jerz *of simple design (P. Costa)*

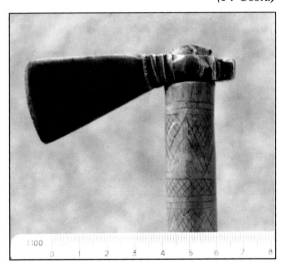

One of the most simple jerz, *resembing a stone implement (P. Costa)*

A jerz *of simple design (P. Costa)*

197

A jerz *of simple design.*
Note the pitting

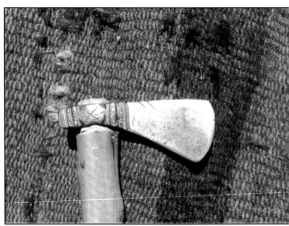

A jerz *of simple design but with*
crude incision

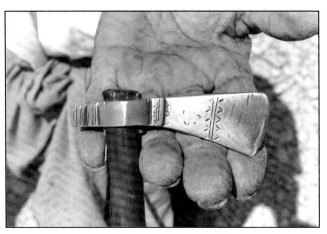

A **worn** jerz *of incised*
design exhibiting a very
simple pattern

A jerz *of incised design with "V"'s.*
Note the brass collar and the silver
head piece

A jerz *of incised design with "V"'s*
enclosed in rough cut lines

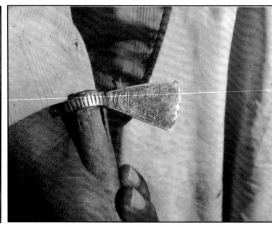

198

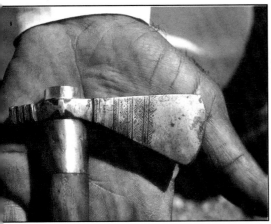

A jerz *of incised design with a crisp pattern and an elongated hammer head*

A jerz *of incised design. It has simple inlay work*

A jerz *of incised design, one of the best examples of the category; note the inlay work and that the design covers about 1/4 of the blade*

A jerz *of incised design, one of the best examples of the category*

A jerz *of inlaid design. Note the rather elongated blade and the jagged end-collar*

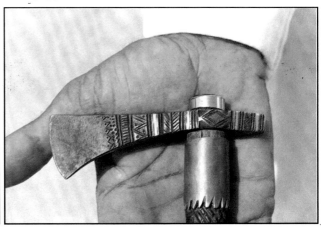

199

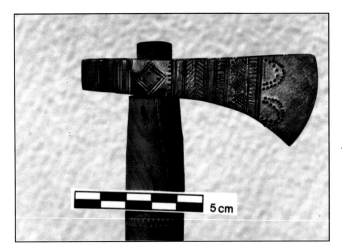

A jerz *of inlaid design*

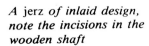

A jerz *of inlaid design,
note the incisions in the
wooden shaft*

A jerz *of inlaid design,
one of the best examples
of this category*

A jerz *of inlaid design, one of the best examples of this category. Note the clear, crisp incisions that fill most of the* jerz. *The inlay work is fine and encircling. The hammer head is indented (courtesy of J. Glover)*

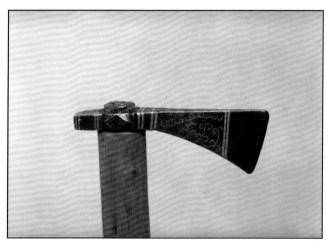

A very personalized jerz *with the name Sayyid Mohammed Qataf inlaid in brass. Note also the 10 lines of inlay (courtesy of C. Berentsen)*

Rashid bin Seif al-Ahamsi of Bayah, the next to last maker of the jerz, *who died in December 1986*

201

A jerz *made currently in Limah*

A jerz *made currently in Limah. Note its similarity to the one which comes from Limah too, but is of a much earlier vintage*

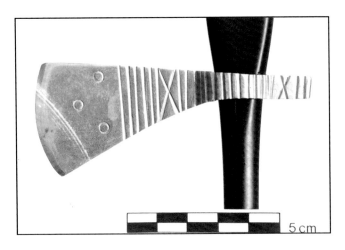

A jerz *currently made in India of standard brass*

A jerz *currently made in Khasab on a forge*

202

Crossed jerz *used as an ornamental feature at a residence in Bukha*

THE MUSANDAM CULTURE

The physical isolation of Musandam is undoubtedly the principal reason for the development of its distinct and uniform culture; this explains also the character of local traditions epitomized by those unique expressions of craftmanship which are the *jerz*, the *bayt al-qufl* and the Kumzari *batil*.

The origin of the jerz may be explained in many ways, perhaps with the help of recent archaeological evidence: it is a fact however that this curious small axe is found nowhere else in Arabia where the dagger is the ubiquitous weapon and symbol of manhood.

Bayt al-qufl, built for a very special way of life is a unique type of construction which displays a strange mixture of primitive and sophisticated features.

The decoration of the boats of the Kamazirah, and especially the zoomorphic stemheads, has no parallel with any other craft, neither in Arabian waters nor in the Indian Ocean.

Indeed Musandam defeats most attempts to find comparisons with other cultures. The relationship between the Musandam habitat and its culture is particularly strong and one must share Vita Finzi's conviction that the history of the region 'has been strongly coloured by its physiographic evolution' (Vita-Finzi 1975:15).

The available data for a history of Musandam and its people and culture are dismally scanty, which is why the historical background prepared for this book is basically an attempt to see facts and events related to Musandam through the history of the neighbouring Gulf countries.

The archaeological reconnaissance promoted by the Royal Geographic Society in 1971 remains to this day the sole archaeological investigation ever conducted in the area. Considering the limited ground covered on that occasion by a one-person team, the results were encouraging and one can well imagine that many things remain concealed in the endless folds of Ru'us al-Jibal, and are bound to be uncovered by future work.

Modern development, normally seen by archaeologists and ecologists as the most destructive element, has provided for Musandam the new motor road which opens up unprecedented opportunities for the study of the region. Built by the Army as a service road, its gravel ribbon develops in a discreet way respecting the environment and the natural beauty of the landscape.

Upper Wadi Bih, near al-Rawdha. Islamic cemetery

Upper Wadi Bih, pre-Islamic cemetery looking towards wadi al-Rawdha

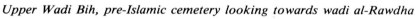

206

No doubt the forbidding terrain and the grandeur of the scenery have themselves been the taming factors which guided and constrained the builders: the result is an amazing and useful artefact which often competes with the natural beauty of the countryside and gives a marvellous means to penetrate an hitherto unknown territory.

At the confluence of the upper Wadi Bih and the short fertile valley of al-Rawdha, right in the heart of the peninsula, the new road has given easy access to a large pre-Islamic necropolis merging into an extensive graveyard of a later period.

The necropolis consists of two rows of seven tombs: one group lies on the eastern bank of the Wadi Bih across the entrance into al-Rawdha; the second along the western side of the wadi, to the south-west of a rocky spur which extends into the valley in a south-easterly direction. On the eastern slope of the hill stands an enigmatic lonely house made of stone blocks of a remarkably large size. Despite the reputation in which this outstanding building is held by the mountain folk, it has been impossible to gather any useful information about its history and function.

The pre-Islamic tombs appear like heaps of loose stones and, without excavation, it is impossible to assess which kind of structure contained the dead. Each tomb may in fact contain multiple burials in one or more parallel chambers.

Although it is clear that the original structures have greatly decayed during thousands of years, through flooding, aeolian erosion and possibly a certain degree of stone robbing, it is highly probable that the original tombs were intentionally

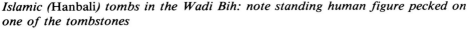

Islamic (Hanbali) tombs in the Wadi Bih: note standing human figure pecked on one of the tombstones

covered by a heap of loose stones. This hypothesis is supported by the fact that not a single ashlar block was found in or around the ruins. The tombs therefore were different from the so-called Umm an-Nar type which was faced with accurately dressed ashlar blocks; rather, they were similar to the cairn tombs described by B. de Cardi (De Cardi 1975: 42-44 and 46-47).

The inner structure of one of the tombs in the eastern Wadi Bih group (the second tomb in the row from the north) was found partly exposed, showing large capstones covering a long narrow chamber occupying the middle of the cairn. Judging from this example and considering the sedimentation which must have built up during the centuries around the tombs, these seem to have been built free -standing above ground.

The Muslim tombs of Wadi Bih and of a second extensive cemetery on a low terrace on the northern side of the wadi leading to the al-Rawdha bowl are marked by large tombstones. The average type is a tall narrow slab, wider at the top and set vertically within a frame of smaller stone blocks. Each tomb is marked by two slabs for a dead male or three for a dead female. Although the slabs have no inscriptions they have the appearance of formal tombstones similar to the inscribed slabs which are normally used in Sunni cemeteries, and differ clearly from the small random stones which are used in the traditional Ibadhi burials.

In more than one case the tombstones of Wadi Bih bear small figures pecked on the front. Since the figures seem to match in size and position the slabs on which they are depicted, it is difficult to explain their presence as existing before the final use of the stone. Instead one can confidently say that the figures have been pecked on the slabs after their use in the graveyard: it is however unclear

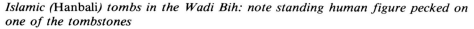

Islamic (Hanbali) tombs in the Wadi Bih: note standing human figure pecked on one of the tombstones

208

whether the figures were casually pecked or were an intentional decoration of the tombstone.

Rock art sites in Musandam have been occasionally reported by travellers and in some cases described by scholars (De Cardi 1975:29), but have not yet been systematically recorded, nor studied at depth and in comparison with other sites of the region and in particular northern Oman. These other sites have been the object of specific studies on the iconographic interpretations and the identification of different styles and techniques (Clark 1976; Preston 1977; Jäckli 1980).

The main concentration of rock art occurs in Wadi Qida, particularly near the inner village set at the head of the valley, where the trackway divides to follow two smaller wadis. The eastern wadi extends several kilometres inland and is inhabited by small communities scattered in several hamlets. The lower Wadi Qida is one of the most fertile areas of Musandam and appears to have a flora even richer than that of Wadi Khasab.

The inner Wadi Qida village consists of some 20-25 houses all of recent construction, being probably modern versions of older houses owned by people who worked abroad and could eventually afford to rebuild their homes. A few remnants of the old settlement can be seen in the area: mostly dry-stone unroofed enclosures with low walls of circular or sub-circular plan. Several old wells are still in use nearby. The valley floor is covered by detrital fill and scatters of large rocks. The petroglyphs are to be found on a group of boulders on a low terrace along the east side of the valley.

The technique is mostly dense pecking or bruising with a pointed stone implement. Usual subjects are animals (goats, sheep and camels); men on horseback armed with spears, bows and possibly shields; boats (*batil* type with single

Tombstone in Wadi Bih with a pecked representation of a date palm (S. Kay)

Horseman, carrying a spear (?) pecked on a boulder in Wadi Qida

and double mast, high stern and small sails). Outlined hands and horned animals of the ibex type are also frequent.

As can be expected boats are common and more accurately depicted at coastal sites, like in the case of Kumzar where a beautiful two-mast vessel is traced with bruised lines. The picture includes a radiating solar disc, repeated twice, perhaps to represent the rising sun.

In general the traditional crafts of Musandam do not have any distinct and outstanding quality of their own and belong to the common repertoire of eastern Arabia which is influenced by the eclectic culture of the Indian Ocean countries.

The iron axe (*jerz*) and some types of pottery are however items of outstanding character.

The diminutive, long-handled axe is undoubtedly a unique implement which has no parallels in Arabia. As far as the present author knows the only other place where it is customary to carry a small axe is among the inhabitants of a few secluded valleys west of Manakha, in northern Yemen (Bani Mansur). Although small, their axe (*fass*) is not as small as the *jerz* and is to be considered mainly a wood cutting tool.

As a wapon the *jerz* could be compared with 'saddle' axes like the *tabarzins* of Iran (Melikian-Chirvani 1979), but the *jerz* is markedly smaller.

The manufacture and decoration of the jerz, described in detail through a number of examples by R.Vincent does not, unfortunately, offer any clues about the origin and history of the axe. Traditional local hardware includes various implements such as spades, ploughshares, sickles and forks. Originally these and other items may have been made by smelting iron from locally mined minerals,

Two-mast boat bruised on the rocks of Kumzar harbour. Note solar disc repeated twice

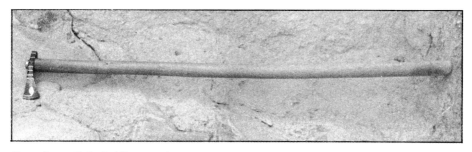

Jerz *from Sal al-A'la*

but at the end of the seventies blacksmiths of Khasab were definitely working only scrap metal (mostly motorcar leaf-springs) or simply retailing imports from India and Pakistan. Second hand *jerz* were occasionally on sale in the suq and coarsely forged *jerz* were available at a blacksmith's shop: I had the impression that simple decoration was left to the taste and file of the customers; a practice which may have been used also in the past. More elaborate ornaments including inlaid brass or other metals was clearly the work of experienced craftsmen: a skill which seems to have long since died in the region.

An exceptional *jerz* was photographed at Sal al-A'la in 1981. The blade fields of this splendid object are decorated with inlaid brass figures: a peacock on one side and two swimming ducks on the other.

The peacock is depicted in a rather stiff and stylized manner which is not mitigated by the realistic presence of the branch, whereas the pair of swimming ducks is a much more lively scene, where an important role is played by the naturalistic detail of the water. (Measures: total lenght 10.8 cm; max. width 3.5 cm; head 1.2 × 1.0 cm).

The peacock is a well known motif of oriental origin which through the Sasanians became common in the late-Roman and medieval art, and is found frequently on Coptic and early Islamic fabrics and brocades. In the Christian iconography it became related to the idea of resurrection and eternity. Symbol of wealth, beauty and regality, probably from the presence of the animal in luxury gardens, the peacock appears in Islamic miniatures and mosaics in idealized representations of heavens and mythical garden scenes. Not surprisingly, therefore, the peacock has remained to this day in the Middle East a popular motif decorating mirrors, boxes, waterpipes and other luxury items. The presence of this animal on a highly symbolic and ceremonial object like the *jerz* is therefore not surprising.

Curious and somewhat difficult to explain are, on the contrary, the two ducks. I must admit that I first judged them as totally alien to the area and therefore suggesting that the object was of foreign manufacture. Later I remembered a relevant and enlightening passage of Wellsted's notes on Musandam. The English traveller, writing about the inhabitants of Khasab and Bukha says: 'They rear a small quantity of poultry within their dwellings, including a few ducks, which I never recollect seeing in any other part of Arabia' (Wellsted 1838:242)

We have thus evidence that ducks existed in Musandam, but were somewhat uncommon domestic animals: this explains their use to decorate the *jerz*.

Pottery displays a distinct local character particularly the large food jars, coffee pots and incense burners produced at Limah, al-Alama and unidentified sites in northern Ra's al-Khaymah.

211

The use of large earthenware containers to store perishable food and water is clearly related to a type of life which involves limited commercial exchanges and long periods of isolation due to difficult communications and wars. Their use has, therefore, become rapidly obsolete within the boundaries of large settlements and in general after changes of living conditions.

Storage of large quantities of food was also a common practice in shaikhly houses and the residences of important tribal chiefs where it was customary to entertain vast numbers of guests, often unexpected and followed by retainers.

In this context it is relevant to notice that jars of an exceptionally large size were recently recovered during restoration works in the castle of Jabrin and in other historic mansions of Oman. The jars, glazed also on the outside, reach an average height of 120 cm. They were possibly produced by Bahla potters in the 17th century A.D.

Judging from the average furniture of the mountain houses (and particularly *bayt al-qufl*), Musandam must have been the last part of Arabia where there has been a widespread use of large pottery containers. This is of course more clearly understood if one bears in mind the kind of life carried on in the isolated mountain settlements, often located far away from sources of water and fresh food. Unlike the Bahla wares, the Musandam storage jars (*fakhhala*) are normally glazed only inside. The fabric is coarse and is either brown-red (from al-Alama) or pale cream (Limah). Light-brown seems the predominant colour of the pots produced in northern Ra's al-Khaymah.

Small incense burners and waterpipe burners are generally made from the very fine red clay of al-Alamah. In the lower Gulf and Oman markets they are known as 'Limah pottery' simply from the name of the port of shipping.

Woodwork has not been examined at any depth. A few items collected for future display in a regional museum have been photographed by R. Vincent with the aim of giving a broader idea of local craftsmanship. Wood is mainly used for utility objects, such as funnels (to fill water-skins, flour bags, etc.) mortars and agricultural tools. Decoration is confined to few items: smoking pipes, beds and doors. Outstanding is a box on four posts preserved in the fort of Khasab: it is one of those portable fire-places which, filled with sand, were used on local boats for limited cooking purposes like grilling kebab and brewing coffee or tea. This fine example has its two long sides decorated in low relief with stylized rosettes and standing animals which include a camel, an ibex and possibly two dogs.

Doors are mostly decorated with circular and interlacing motifs obtained with the use of dividers. The various patterns depend on the size and shape of a few carving tools which leave clear marks in the sharp and crisp carving.

In general the decoration is made by linear tracing of simple motifs: carving is very limited and never creates a low relief of plastic quality. It is interesting to note that local boats do not bear any carved decoration, and, as we have seen, ornament is obtained by applied goatskins and shells. Musandam seems, therefore, to lack the presence of those artisans who in other maritime communities along the coast of Oman carry out boat-building and other carpentry works which involve a developed type of wood-carving (Costa-Kite 1985:146).

The architecture of Musandam of both mountain and coast types may be defined as a 'spontaneous' way of building. As is the case in general for the 'architecture without architects' (to borrow Bernard Rudofsky's happy definition) one would expect to find in Musandam, like for example in the Yemen, a great variety of technical solutions, details and features reflecting the personality of each mason. Local buildings display on the contrary a totally different charac-

Storage jar in a ruined house at Sasaha, al-Rawdha

Storage jars and cooking pots in a house of Sal al-A'la. Note glazed jar in the left corner, covered by a large flat-rimmed bowl

House of a 'Lower Gulf' type in Wadi Qida

ter: within each of the two environmental sub-divisions an absolute uniformity predominates which excludes any variation and makes no concession to individuality. It would however be wrong to conclude that the adoption of a single house-form must inevitably result in a dull and unpleasant built environment: in the mountains the adaptation of buildings as well as living areas to the irregular terrain is enough to break monotony and attractively articulate the settlement layout, while the position on different levels helps to ensure privacy and definition to each dwelling complex.

On the coast a number of odd and unexpected building may occasionally be found: these are however to be seen as eccentric imports due to overseas contacts and not as internal variations of the local architecture. Like a Swiss chalet in San Giminiano they do not break the general uniformity of style and strict relationship of the built environment with the climate and socio-economic organization.

Local architecture is undoubtedly marked by peculiar regional characteristics which, as we have seen, originate from the extreme isolation of the country, the secluded and endogamous type of society, the harsh habitat and finally the limited availability of building materials, a problem worsened by extremely difficult communications both along the steep coasts and through the rugged hinterland.

Despite all this the architecture, especially on the coast, uses a vocabulary which belongs to a region which exceeds the limits of Musandam itself and stretches to both sides of the Gulf littoral and beyond.

The traditional mosque of the coast, (well represented by the Great Mosque of Bukha) and of which examples are preserved at Khasab, Limah and Dibah-Bayah, has the following peculiarities:

Bukha, the Great Mosque

— *Plan.* The prayer hall is formed by a number of transverse aisles preceded by a single aisle portico and a small forecourt.
— *Mihrab.* A deep mihrab niche protruding on the outside; small windows; if a built and recessed minbar exists there is no communication between the two;
— *Roofing.* The mosque is covered by a flat roof supported by pillars with or without arches parallel to the *qibla* wall.
— *Minaret.* No minaret exists; in a few cases the 'staircase minaret' can be found.

The type of mosque summarily outlined above has many features in common with the average mosque of the Arabian littoral, from Kuwait to Sur, but also with buildings of the Irano-Baluchi shores and of East Africa (Lewcock-Freeth 1978:25; Hardy-Guilbert 1980:112-113; King 1986:168-188).

The unique building which is *bayt al-qufl*, shares a number of features with

216

Bayt al-qufl *in the hinterland of Khasab (axe handle 82 cm long)*

building types of neighbouring areas, particularly the 'sunken house' of the northern Hajar (Costa-Wilkinson 1987: 221). Humbler, temporary shelters like the *musayf* huts of the Kamazirah can be found in other parts of northern Oman well outside the Musandam region, as for example in the Batinah where a large group of huts in a palm-grove at al-Junaynah near Barka is built in the same manner (Costa 1985:118). This can of course be explained by the immigration of groups of Kamazirah into the Batinah, but it would also imply that Musandam people had external contacts while maintaining their own building traditions.

It is, on the other hand, surprising not to find within Musandam any trace of the pitched-roof house (*karijin*) typical not only of the Batinah (Costa 1985:117 ff.) and of the northern Hajar (Costa- Wilkinson 1987:220) but also of northern Ra's al-Khaymah (Dostal 1983, passim)

On the coasts a more eclectic type of architecture occurs and even plaster decoration shows analogies with other areas: the 'horned' pattern which is visible in the fort of Khasab is a common motif in the arch decoration at Umm al-Qaiwayn and Ajman and indeed in the Mughal-derived architecture along the Indian Ocean shores.

In general all the buildings which have been considered in this study show little or no evidence of conceptual planning. The mosque layout involves a repetition of roofed units parallel to the qibla wall: a simple scheme which can meet any space requirement by simply adding more units to a basic plan which consists of a roofed room in front of the mihrab, an ablution area and a courtyard linking the two and at the same time separating the mosque from the street.

The portico, however, which is apparently only an extra unit separated from the prayer hall, is in fact a relevant conceptual step forward in the evolution of

217

Khasab fort, stucco decoration above one of the doors

Khasab, Masjid al-Khor, a small mosque which once stood near the NW tower of the fort

Chicken house of bayt al-qufl *type. Note slab and stone used to block entrance during the night*

the basic building scheme described above. The plan of the mosque with a portico results, in fact, from a broad overall foresight of the visual and functional requirements of the building. It is interesting to note that a single or a double aisled portico is common in the traditional mosques of Qatar (Hardy-Guilbert 1980: 112-115), the eastern coast of Oman and the Dhofar littoral (Costa-Kite 1985): a vast cultural area of which Musandam is clearly a part. Surprisingly the stepped wall leading to the roof, noticed as an important feature of the Bukha mosque, has parallels in inner Oman, at Imti and Nizwa, the heartland of the Ibadi territory (Costa: forthcoming).

In the mountain settlements mosques are small buildings lacking any special external feature or identification. Made inconspicuous by the construction methods and materials used locally, the building often goes unnoticed by strangers. This is probably why some travellers have remarked that there is a general lack of mosques in the Musandam interior and why B. Thomas can state that 'though they build no mosques in the mountains and their knowledge of religion may not be profound, they are Muslims' (Thomas 1929:80).

The average mountain mosque is the size of a normal house, totally built above ground, with one entrance: it is practically an open building provided only with a light door to keep animals out. The only feature of identification is the *mihrab* which is however fairly small and has often the appearance of a domestic wall-niche. The only identification of the *mihrab* is the pointed arch formed by two stone slabs set at a 90 degree angle.

Most of these mosques are built with stone from foundations to roof, but walls are thinner than the average domestic structure and less strongly built. Mosques with palm-frond or acacia branch upper structures on stone lower walls

Ruined mosque at Sayh, near Jabal Harim

Rural mosque in the upper Wadi Bih

Masonry plinth, said to be traditionally used for call to prayer along an ancient track in the massif of Jabal Harim

are not uncommon both in the mountains and the western coast areas (Dostal 1983: 47, pl.24).

Both building types described above have parallels outside the Musandam area: the stone mosque with pointed arched *mihrab* is common in the Jabal al-Akhdhar and in the inner Hajar al-Gharbi valleys (Costa: forthcoming), whereas the mosque made of palm-frond on stone structure occurs in the Wadi al-Jizzi area (Costa-Wilkinson 1987:108 and 220).

Many traditional customs of Musandam appear to be basically common throughout Arabia. The *khayr*, (the water jar for public use previously described) is a pious gesture which increases the social prestige of the donor. It is comparable with the Arabian *sabil* particularly common in the Yemen, or, with the construction of a *falaj* or a well with adjoining cistern for the use of travellers (*waqbah*) which in Oman are often constructed with individual or single family money for the benefit of the community (Costa 1983:290-94; Costa-Kite 1985: 151).

In summary, a wider look at the problem of the origin and development of the many building types of Musandam reveals that the radius of their expansion is much larger than the present knowledge of the vernacular architecture of eastern Arabia seems to suggest. The only exception is *bayt al-qufl*, the most extraordinary and unique building in the Arabian peninsula.

Yet, between the barren land of the 'fish-eaters' in the west and the multi-faceted economy of the fertile Batinah plain in the east, Musandam stands out as a distinct enclave both physically and socio-economically, where a small population developed remarkable skills for a combined use of the limited available resources: an achievement which is reflected in the special features of the local material culture and architecture that this book has attempted to present.

The silt plain of Sayh with the Jabal Harim in the background (R.K. Vincent Jr.)

Khor Niyad, looking north towards the Strait of Hormuz

Khor Khasab at high tide. After the development of recent years this scenery has greatly changed: a surfaced road now follows the coast; the little mosque by the beach has been removed and modern port facilities have been built on the western side of the bay

223

The bay of Qida and the small inlet of Mukhi, to the west of Khasab. The new road is under construction: in the foreground a sambuk *carrying a fish trap is moored by the coast (G. Crocker)*

New and old at Kumzar (G. Crocker)

Army road to Musandam in the hinterland of Diba/Bayah (1981)

The bay of Bukha from the jetty

Pre-Islamic tombs in the upper Wadi Bih

Islamic Hanbali cemetery in the wadi leading to al-Rawdha

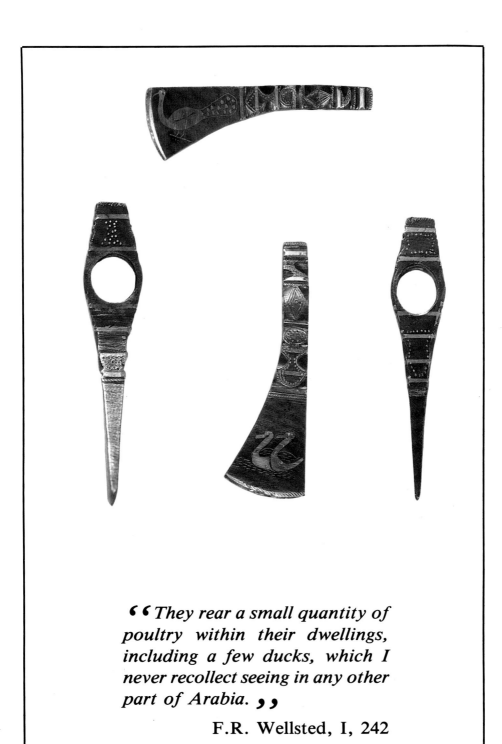

" They rear a small quantity of poultry within their dwellings, including a few ducks, which I never recollect seeing in any other part of Arabia. "

F.R. Wellsted, I, 242

Jerz from Sal al-A'la. Iron with inlaid brass decoration including on one side of the blade a peacock resting on a bar and on the other side two swimming ducks. The stylized rendering of the peacock contrasts with the lively representation of the ducks

Cooking pot from Limah. The ocre-pink fabric is decorated with floral motifs painted in red and incised lines obtained with a comb. The vase bottom, raised to four protruding points, shows the clear inprint of the cloth used by the potter to mould the lower part of the pot. The upper part is hand-made (G. Crocker)

Coffee pot with flattened globular body, a high tapering neck, one handle and a long raised spout. Handle and spout are connected by a sharp-edged rib. The colour is dark-ochre with groups of vertical red lines. Incised grooves decorate the handle (G. Crocker)

Incense burners and a water-pipe burner made by al-Alama potters (G. Crocker)

Wooden fire-box. Two sides of the frame are decorated with carved figures which include an ibex, a camel, a horse and a fourth animal, possibly a dog. Filled with sand these boxes were used on boats for limited cooking purposes like brewing coffee or tea and grilling kebabs

Houses of the coastal village of Qida, displaying non-local features

The small khor *mosque of Khasab. This building, no longer existing, belonged to the portico type, common on the Gulf shores*

Tower-house of the mountain village of Sabtayn: a unique example of development of bayt al-qufl *type*

The great mosque of Khasab, a relatively late building which incorporates traditional architectural features

Traditional bayt al-qufl *of Sal al-A'la*

Close-up of Shaykh Masud shrine on the northern coast of Musandam

REFERENCES

Abu-Hakima, Ahmed Mustafa
1965, *History of eastern Arabia, 1750-1800*. Beirut.

Ash T.
1978, *An introduction to the archaeology, ethnography and history of Ra's al-Kheyma*. National Museum Ra's al-Kheyma.

Aubin J.
1972, "Le royaume de Hormuz au debut du xvi siecle", *Mare Luso-Indicum II*, pp.77-179.

Badger G.P.
1871, *History of the Imams and Seyyds of Oman*, by Salil Ibn Raziq from A.D. 661 to 1856. London.

Baizerman S., Searle K.
1978, *Finishes in the Ethnic Tradition*. U.S.A.: Dos Tejedoras.

Bosch D. and S.
1982, *Seashells of Oman*. London: Longman.

Bathurst R.D.
1967, *The Ya'rubi dinasty of Oman*, unpublished Ph.D. thesis.

Boucharlat R., Salles J.F.
1981, "The history and archaeology of the Gulf from the 5th century B.C. to the 7th century A.D.". *Seminar for Arabian Studies*, pp.65-94

Boxer C.R.
rep. 1985, *Portuguese conquest and commerce in southeastern Asia. 1500-1750*: "Anglo-Portuguese rivalry in the Persian Gulf 1615-1635".

Butler A.
1979, *The Batsford Encyclopaedia of Embroidery Stitches*. London.

Casson L.
1989, *The Periplus Maris Erithraei*. Princeton.

Clark C.
1976, "The rock art of Oman", *Journal of Oman Studies* 1, pp. 113-122

Cleuziou S.
1985, "Zwischen Sumer und Meluchcha: Magan". *Das Altertum* Bd. 31,3 pp.141-150.

Cleuziou S.
1986, "Dilmun and Makan during the 3rd millennium and early 2nd millennium. A tentative review". *Bahrein through the Ages*, pp.143-156.

Coles A., Jackson P.
1975, *A wind-tower house in Dubai*. London

Collingwood P.
1987, *Textile and Weaving Structures*. London.

Cornelius P.F.S., Falcon N.L., South D., Vita Finzi C.
1973, "The Musandam Expedition 1971-72. Scientific Results" *Geographical Journal* 139, pp 400-425

Crocker G.
1982. The Traditional and Current State of the Art of Weaving in the Country Oman at Large and in the Pastoral Community in Particular. *In: U.N. Project No. OMA/80/W01* (Unpublished).

Crocker G.
1983, "Omani Weaving since the Production of Oil". *The Journal for Weavers, Spinners and Dyers*. London.

Crocker G.
1986, Omani Weaving in the 1980s. *The Journal for Weavers, Spinners and Dyers*, London.

Crowfoot G.M.
1943. "Handicrafts in Palestine". *Palestine Exploration Quarterly*, July-October.

Costa, P.M.
1988 "Pre-islamic Izki: some field evidence" *P.S.A.S.*, 18, pp. 15-23

Costa P.M.
1983, "Notes on the traditional hydraulics and agriculture in Oman", *World Archeology* pp. 273-295

Costa P.M.
1985, "The *sur* of the the Batinah". *Journal of Oman Studies* 8,2, pp.121-193

Costa P.M., Kite S.
1985, "Notes on the architecture of Salalah and the Dhofar littoral", *Journal of Oman Studies* 7, pp. 131-153

Costa P.M., Wilkinson T.J.
1987, "The hinterland of Sohar", *Journal of Oman Studies* 9, pp. 1-238

De Cardi B.
1975, "Archaelogical survey in Northern Oman", *East and West*, 25, 1-2 pp. 9-75

De Cardi B.
1973, "A Sasanian outpost in Northern Oman", *Antiquity* pp.305-310.

De Cardi B.
1975, "Archaeological survey in Northern Oman 1972", *East and West*, pp.9-76.

Donaldson P.
1984, "Prehistoric tombs of Ra's al Kheima", *Oriens Antiquus* 3-4, pp.193-280.

Dostal W.
1972, "The Shihuh of Northern Oman. A contribution to cultural ecology", *Geographical Journal*, 138, pp. 1-7

Dostal W.
1983, *Traditional architecture of Ra's al Khaymah North*. Wiesbaden.

Eilers W.
1983, "Das Volk der Maka vor nach der Achaemeniden" AMI Erganzungsband 10, pp.101-119.

Emery I.
1980, *The Primary Structures of Fabrics*. Washington, D.C.: The Textile Museum.

Ezzah A.
1979, "The political situation in Eastern Arabia at the advent of Islam", *Seminar for Arabian Studies*, pp.53-64.

Falcon N.L.
1972, "Expedition to unknown Musandam", *Geographical Magazine*, pp. 105-111.

Falcon N.L.
1973. "The Musandam (Northern Oman) expedition 1971-72 *Geographical Journal* 139, pp 1-19

Fiorani Piacentini V.
1975, *L'emporio ed il regno di Hormoz.*

Foster W.
1933, *England's quest of eastern trade.* London.

Gallagher M., Woodcock M.W.
1980, *The birds of Oman.* London.

Hardy-Guilbert C.
1980, "Recherches sur la Periode islamique au Qatar", *Mission Archeologique Française au Qatar* pp. 111-127

Hardy-Guilbert C., Lalande C.
1981, *La maison de Shaykh 'Isa à Bahreyn.* Paris.

Harris Phelps C.
1969, "The Persian Gulf submarine telegraph", *Geographical Journal* 135,2, pp.169-190.

Hart C. and D.
1976, *Natural Baskertry.* New York.

Hasan H.
1928, *A history of Persian navigation.* London.

Heard-Bey F.
1982, *From Trucial States to United Arab Emirates.* London, New York.
Heyerdhal T.
1980, *The Tigris expedition.* London.

Holdgate C.
1970, *Netmaking for All.* London.

Hourani G.F.
1951, *Arab seafaring in the Indian Ocean in ancient and early medieval times.* Princeton.

Jäckli R.
1980, *Rock art in Oman. An introductory presentation.* Zug.

King G.R.
1986, *The historical mosques of Saudi Arabia.* London.

Krause R.F.
1983, *Die Bedeutungverschiebungen Omanischer Hafenstädte und Wandlungstendenzen im Omanischer Seehandel in den letzten 1500 Jahren.* Würzburg.

Landen R.G.
1967, *Oman since 1856*. Princeton.

Lewcock R.B., Freeth Z.
1978, *Traditional architecture in Kuwait and the northern Gulf*. London AARP.

Lorimer J.G.
1908-1915, *Gazetteer of the Persian Gulf, Oman and Central Arabia*. Calcutta.

Lowick N.
1974, "Trade patterns on the Persian Gulf in the light of recent coin evidence", *Studies in honour of G. Miles*, D. Kouymjian, ed. Beirut.

Mandaville J.P.
1978, Wild Flowers of Northern Oman. Bromley.

Mandaville J.P. Jr.
1985, "A botanical reconnaissance in the Musandam region in Oman" *Journal of Oman Studies* 7, pp. 9-28.

Melikian Chirvani A.S.
1979, "The Tabarzins of Lotf 'Ali" in: Elgod R., ed., *Islamic arms and armours*. London.

al-Murshid al-'ām li al-wilāt wa al-gaba' il fi Sultạnat 'Umān. Muscat 1402/1982.

Miles S.B.
1919, *The countries and tribes of the Persian Gulf*. London.

Pettinato G.
1972, "Il commercio con l'estero della Mesopotamia meridionale nel 3 millennio a.C. alla luce delle fonti letterarie lessicali sumeriche", *Mesopotamia* VII.

Potts D.
1978, "Towards an integrated history of culture change in the Arabian Gulf area: notes on Dilmun, Makkan and the economy of ancient Sumer", *Journal of Oman Studies* 4, pp.29-51.

Potts D.
1985, "From Qade to Mazun: four notes on Oman, c. 700 B.C. to 700 A.D.", *Journal of Oman Studies* 8,1, pp.81-95.

Potts D.
1986, "The booty of Magan", *Oriens Antiquus* xxv, 3-4, pp.271-285.

Preston K.
1976, "An introduction to the anthropomorphic content of the rock art of the Jebel al Akhdar", *Journal of Oman Studies* 2, pp.17-38.
1967, *Red Sea and Gulf of Aden Pilot, Admiralty*. London.

Richards D.S., ed.
1970, *Islam and the trade of Asia*. Oxford.

Ricks T.M.
1970, "Persian Gulf seafaring and East Africa, IX-XII century." *African Historical Studies*, pp.339-357.

Rudofsky B.
1964, *Architecture without architects*. London.

Rudofsky B.
1977, *The prodigious builders*. New York, London.

Schoff W. (tr. and ed.)
1912, *The Periplus of the Erythraean Sea*. New York.

Serjeant R.B.
1978, "Historical sketch of the Gulf in the Islamic era", in: *Qatar Archaeological Report 1973*, pp.147-163.

Sirhan b. Said b. Sirhan
rep. 1984, *Annals of Oman*, trans. and annotated by E.C. Ross, Cambridge.

Smith S.
1954, "Events in Arabia in the 6th century A.D.", *Bulletin of the School of Oriental and African Studies*, 3, pp.425-468.

Speiser N.
1983, *The Manual of Braiding*. Basel.

Stone F., ed.
1985, *Studies on the Tihamah*. London.

Thomas B.
1929, "The Musandam Peninsula and its people the Shihuh", *Journal of the Royal Asiatic Society*, pp.71-86.

Thomas B.,
1930, *The kumzari Dialect of the Shihuh tribe, Arabia*. Asiatic Society Monographs xxi.

Thomas B.S.
1931, *Alarms and excursions in Arabia*. Indianapolis.

Tosi M.
1986, "Early maritime cultures of the Arabian Gulf and the Indian Ocean", *Bahrein through the Ages*, pp.94-107.

Vita Finzi C.
1982, "Recent coastal deformation near the Strait of Hormuz", *Proceedings of the Royal Geographic Society*, London, pp.441-457.

Vita Finzi C., Cornelius P.F.S.
1973, "Cliff sapping by molluscs in Oman'" *Journal of Sedimentary Petrology*, 43,1, pp.31-32.

Wellsted J.R.
1838, *Travels in Arabia*. London.

Wilkinson J.C.
1964, "A sketch of the historical geography of the Trucial Oman down to the beginning of the 16th century", *Geographical Journal* 130, pp.337-449.

Wilkinson J.C.
1973, "Arab-Persian relationship in late Sasanian Oman", *Seminar for Arabian Studies* pp.40-51.

Wilkinson J.C.
1982, "The early development of the Ibadi movement in Basra", in: *Studies in the first century of Islamic Society, G.H.A. Juynboll, ed.* Southern Illinois University Press, pp.125-144.

Wilkinson J.C.
1987, *The Imamate tradition of Oman.* Cambridge.

Whitehouse D.
1979, "Maritime trade in the Arabian Sea", *South Asian Archaeology 1977*, pp.865-885.

Whitehouse D., Williamson A.
1973, "Sasanian maritime trade", *Iran* XI, pp.29-49.

Williamson A.
1973, "Hormuz and the trade of the Gulf in the 14th-15th cen. A.D.", *Seminar for Arabian Studies*, pp.52-68.

Wilson A.T.
1928, *The Persian Gulf.* Oxford.

Zimmermann W.
1981, "Die Beduinen von Musandam im Sultanat Oman", in: Scholtz F. ed., *Beduinen im Zeichen des Erdöls.* Weisbaden.

INDEX

246

Minab river 43
Minbar 75
Ming pottery 58
Moluccas 49
Mongol rulers 46
Mosque 215-216, 217, 220
Mshak see pottery decoration
Musandam Development Committee 57
Musayf see hut
Muscat 80

Nadir Shah 51, 52
Nasaa see braiding
Nasir bin Murshid 50, 51
Nets 151, 180
Netting needle, 180
Niniveh 42
Nubia 42

Pakistan 195, 210
Palm
    frond rib *zura*, 171
    inflorescence, *esqa* 174
Parthians 42
Periplus of the Erythraen Sea 42, 43, 57
Plaster, hydraulic, *saruj* 75
Pliny 42, 43, 45
Portuguese 16, 48-51, 60
Pottery 151-152, 183-185, 211-212
    decoration, *mshak*, 152, 183
Pot
    coffee 183
    cooking 183
    for ghee 184
Ptolemy 42
Punjab

Qade 42
Qais 46
Qajar empire 64
Qalhat 47
Qarmathians 45
Qatif 43, 46
Qawasim 52, 54
Qida 27
Qishm 28
Qidfa 191, 195

Qufl, lock
    alaq 98, 100
    malaqa 98
    zalq 100, 101

Raghwa see whorl
Ra's al-Khaymah 18, 28, 45, 211, 212
Ra's al-Sham 25
Ra's Sheikh Mas'ud 118
Raqam see drum decoration
Rawdha 207
Rock art 208, 209, 210
Rope, *habl* 175
Royal Geographic Society Expedition 37, 117, 205
Ru'us al-Jibal 48, 205
Rubi 103, 106-111
Run-off irrigation 27, 123
Rustaq 43

Sabkha 18
Sabtayn 124
Saddle, *shidah* 179
    cloth, *bardaa* 178
Saffah ventilated room 109
Sal al-A'la 106, 112, 114, 117
Sal al-Asfal 115, 118
Saruj, hydraulic plaster, 75
Sasanian domination 43-45
    pottery 58
    ruins 15, 44
Seasonal migration, *takhwil* 17, 95
Seljuks 45, 46
Shabankara'i 46
Shah Abbas 51
Shapur II 43
Shihr 43
Shihuh 27, 57, 67, 95
Sibta 175
Siraf 44, 45
Skin containers 152
Sohar 43, 45
Spindle, *maghzal* 177
Spinning 149, 177
Stitching 166
Suez canal 53
Sumatra 49
Sumerians 41
Sur al-kamazirah 59

**Graphic design
by Eraldo Rosina**

Printed in Italy
June 1991
by industria grafica GIGLIO
Scafati (Salerno)